Perestroika in Eastern Europe

Perestroika in Eastern Europe

Hungary's Economic Transformation, 1945–1988

Gábor Révész

with a Foreword by Paul Marer

Westview Press
BOULDER, SAN FRANCISCO, & LONDON

Westview Special Studies on the Soviet Union and Eastern Europe

This Westview softcover edition is printed on acid-free paper and bound in library-quality, coated covers that carry the highest rating of the National Association of State Textbook Administrators, in consultation with the Association of American Publishers and the Book Manufacturers' Institute.

Copyright © 1990 by Westview Press, Inc.

Published in 1990 in the United States of America by Westview Press, Inc., 5500 Central Avenue, Boulder, Colorado 80301, and in the United Kingdom by Westview Press, Inc., 13 Brunswick Centre, London WC1N 1AF, England

Library of Congress Cataloging-in-Publication Data
Révész, G. (Gábor)
   Perestroika in Eastern Europe : Hungary's economic transformation,
1945–1988 / Gábor Révész ; with a foreword by Paul Marer.
      p. cm. — (Westview special studies on the Soviet Union and
Eastern Europe)
   Includes bibliographical references.
   ISBN 0-8133-7752-8
   1. Hungary—Economic policy—1945– . 2. Central planning—Hungary.
3. Perestroïka. I. Title. II. Series.
HC300.28.R48   1990
338.9439′009′045—dc20   89-37019
                                                                 CIP

Printed and bound in the United States of America

The paper used in this publication meets the requirements of the American National Standard for Permanence of Paper for Printed Library Materials Z39.48-1984.

10   9   8   7   6   5   4   3   2

Contents

Tables and Figures

Foreword

Among the countries that have had a centrally planned economic and communist political system and have remained in the Soviet sphere of influence, Hungary has been—and remains—a pioneer in pursuing economic and political reforms. Hungary's reform experiment, now more than twenty years old, has been both fascinating and historically important.

The historical importance of Hungary's experiment is, in my view, threefold. One reason is the lesson that it teaches us about one of the great and as yet not fully settled questions in comparative systems: Is efficient market socialism a realistic possibility? (I define "efficient market socialism" as [1] a well-performing and substantially market-driven economy in which [2] the means of production remain predominantly non-private, [3] the government assumes responsibility for an economic policy that substantially circumscribes economic activities, [4] the distribution of income and wealth is relatively egalitarian, and [5] the political party that governs is firmly committed to these four economic principles.) The experience of Hungary suggests that the answer may well be negative, certainly until the ownership issue is resolved in a way that is consistent with market efficiency.

The further historical importance of the Hungarian experiment lies in the fact that it suggests that the dynamics of the reform processes in centrally planned economies have certain common and predictable intellectual, political, and bureaucratic features. Although no two countries are alike in their environments and policies, there is much that reformers of centrally planned economies—and outside observers of the reform process—can learn from Hungary's experience as they try to shape, and we in the West attempt to understand and predict, future developments in the Soviet Union, Poland, and elsewhere. As the author himself states at the beginning of Chapter 8:

> It is worth noting that the very successful changes adopted in China in the 1980s were in many ways based on the Hungarian experience; likewise, Gorbachev's *perestroika* and the subsequent economic renewal in several Eastern European countries have numerous points in common with events

that began in Hungary some twenty years ago. The mistakes and the fact that Hungary's reform was halted at one stage may also prove instructive.

An even more important lesson of the Hungarian experiment is that as long as real market pressures—and opportunities to excel by offering superior products—remain limited by pervasive government intervention in the economy, progress will be halting, so that even a "reformed" country like Hungary will fall further and further behind the newly industrializing and already industrialized market-economy countries. Whether Hungary can break out of its present predicament by "escaping forward" is a question that is crucial—but very difficult to answer.

Perhaps the greatest historical significance of Hungary's reform experiment is the substantial direct impact that the outcome of its reform-cum-transformation will have on political and economic developments in the USSR and elsewhere in Eastern Europe. If the Hungarian experiment is associated with sustained political instability and deteriorating economic performance—a distinct possibility—that fact will certainly weaken the reform program of Gorbachev and those of his like-minded colleagues in the USSR and in the other Eastern European countries. Conversely, if—after a period of transition—the Hungarian experiment leads to political stability under a more democratic political system as well as to sustained improvements in economic performance, that fact will surely boost the positions of the reformers elsewhere.

Western assessments of Hungary's reform experiment have been somewhat superficial and faddish. From the late 1960s until the mid-1980s, the Hungarian experiment was evaluated in the West much too favorably. In recent years, when many hitherto hidden problems have surfaced, Western comments have tended toward the opposite extreme, pronouncing the Hungarian experiment a failure.

We are fortunate to have in hand this objective account and balanced assessment of Hungary's reform experiment. This book is a valuable addition to the meager literature available in the English language on Hungary's reform process and results. It is an account by an "insider" who has superb knowledge of the facts and an ability to take a detached, independent, academic view of the unfolding reform process.

The author, Gábor Révész, is one of Hungary's distinguished economists. During his forty-year career, he has worn a variety of hats. For about two decades (1949–1967), he held a series of positions in Hungary's state economic administration: in the Ministry of Finance, at the Investment Bank, and in the National Planning Office. He served also as a member of the committee of experts that prepared the New Economic Mechanism introduced in 1968. Early on in his career, Dr. Révész began teaching economics at various colleges and universities in Hungary (an activity he still continues), and he has made guest appearances abroad, in the East, and also in the West. Since 1967, his principal position has been that of a senior research economist at the Institute of Economics of the Hungarian Academy of Sciences, where his research has focused on broad questions of reform strategy, especially on labor and compensation issues. Dr. Révész is the author of numerous publications; some of them have appeared in English.

This book was completed in November 1988, just about the time when Hungary was entering a new and accelerated phase in its economic and political reform process. Although Chapter 7 sketches some of the fascinating new developments that took place during 1987 and 1988, giving the reader a sense of the dramatic events that were unfolding in Hungary at that time, the author is obviously not in a position to make an assessment that is fully up-to-date and definitive. Attempting such an assessment will be the task of economic historians for years.

Even people who are experts on the economic mechanisms and policies of centrally planned economies may not have a good "feel" for what it is like to live in a socialist country. To fill this gap, the author has included a nontechnical, snapshot description of life in contemporary Hungary: what Hungarians and foreign visitors find in the shops and restaurants; in what areas the "market" works; health care, child care, and the educational system; private farming and other "second economy" activities; how a typical family earns and spends its income; and the nature and extent of wealth and poverty in the country.

Thus, *Perestroika in Eastern Europe* is one of those rare books that can be read with profit by laypersons who want to know more about what economic life is like in a partially reformed "socialist" Eastern European country as well as by economists, political scientists, sociologists, and historians interested in Eastern Europe or in the political-economic transformation of communist societies.

Paul Marer
Bloomington, Indiana

Preface

This book discusses the operational system of the Hungarian economy and its changes since World War II, with social and political developments in the background. The title, though it refers to Eastern Europe, is not misleading.

In historical perspective, we are witnessing the last days of the classical (Stalinist) model of a socialist economic system based on plan directives. This model took shape in the Soviet Union in the 1930s and was adopted by the Eastern European countries that found themselves in that country's sphere of influence after the war as a result of the Yalta Conference.[1] At the end of the 1980s, it was being more or less clearly recognized not only by the populations but also by the authorities in several Eastern European countries that the present system is unable to ensure the rational management of those economies—in particular, their effective integration into the international division of labor—and hence the system cannot meet the social and individual demands of the populations. Consequently, the adoption of a modern market economy and a corresponding political reorganization have become fundamental issues in these countries, as has become evident not only in Hungary but also in Poland and the German Democratic Republic.

Hungary, in a sense, has been a guinea pig in the historical transformation in Eastern Europe. The country's first reform steps toward a market economy were taken in the second part of the 1960s, but external pressures and internal opposition derailed that reform process and led to mistaken decisions in economic policy. However, Hungary stands alone among the Comecon countries[2] in having rid itself of plan directives. The Hungarian story may therefore be viewed as a precedent. Similar questions and proposals, difficulties and social tensions, counteractions and obstacles have appeared and will appear in Poland and the Soviet Union—and at some future date, in the other, "more dormant" socialist countries also. Thus, in relating the Hungarian story, this book forecasts the trends of the coming changes and conflicts in the rest of Eastern Europe.

The book consists of eight chapters. The first one is intended to introduce Hungary to the reader, and it must be emphasized that the material in this chapter reflects the situation as it was in 1986; living standards and the general economic situation have worsened considerably since then (as detailed in Chapter 7). Chapters 2 and 3 outline the introduction of the Stalinist economic and political model in Hungary and describe its operation from the postwar era through 1967. Chapters 4–6 discuss the economic reforms of 1968, their petering out, the mistaken decisions of economic policy, and the consequences of all of these factors for economic performance and the reform process. Chapter 7 describes the situation in 1987 and 1988. The dramatic acceleration of political changes is indicated through a number of news items, and this chapter also calls attention to important new legislation (e.g., tax and company laws) and other measures that may establish the preconditions of a mixed market economy. The last chapter sums up the process of "deformation" of the reforms and discusses the chances of a breakthrough.

The book relies primarily upon Hungarian economic literature. I have tried to refer to the most important studies, knowing full well the subjectivity of any choice given the enormous body of rich literature on the topic. A separate Additional Readings section lists selected publications on the Hungarian economy in English, together with a few works in German and French. Most of the data in the book came from official Hungarian statistics, which are considered by most specialists to be reliable in the sense that the gaps and biases are about on a par with those of the official statistics of highly developed countries.[3]

In 1984 and 1986, I spent a few months in the United States lecturing at universities about Hungary's reforms. On reading the texts of my lectures, my newly found friends, Pearl and Roy Bennett, suggested that I convert these lectures into a book for Americans. In the following pages I have tried to do just that.

I owe the Bennetts thanks for their suggestions concerning the construction of the book. I owe them further thanks for arranging that a rough translation of this manuscript be turned into standard English and thus into a more readable text. I also wish to thank Paul Marer, Professor at Indiana University, and Susan McEachern, Senior Editor at Westview Press, for their encouragement, editorial suggestions, and assistance with the publication of this book. Several of my Hungarian colleagues and friends read the original manuscript; for their comments and stimulating observations my thanks go to László Antal, Tamás Bauer, György Csáki, Eva Ehrlich, Róbert Hock, László Kahulits, Sándor Kopátsy, Tamás Nagy, András Révész, and Aladár Sipos.

Gábor Révész
Budapest, Hungary

Notes

1. A 1945 conference attended by the heads of state of the United States, the United Kingdom, and the USSR at which it was agreed, among other things, that the Eastern European countries would belong to the Soviet sphere of influence.

2. Council for Mutual Economic Assistance (also CMEA), whose members include Bulgaria, Czechoslovakia, the German Democratic Republic, Hungary, Poland, Romania, the USSR, Vietnam, Mongolia, and Cuba.

3. In the mid-1960s, the Central Statistical Office of Hungary revised the country's postwar macroeconomic statistics; since then the revised data have appeared in long-time series.

1

Impressions

This book explores the economic system established in Hungary since 1948–1949. The main features of this system as it had evolved by the mid-1980s can be stated briefly:

- There is a one-party system in the country. From 1948 to 1956 the ruling communist party was known as the Hungarian Labor party; in November 1956 the name was changed to the Hungarian Socialist Workers' party.
- Most of the means of production are in public hands, owned by the state or by cooperatives.
- Nevertheless, the private sector accounts for a large share of production and distribution, mainly in the form of small businesses that are only partly or formally attached to the large socialist enterprises. These small entrepreneurs produce an estimated one-third of Hungary's gross national product (GNP) and dominate in some types of goods and services.
- The provision of goods and services is controlled by the market, not by so-called plan directives that typify the other socialist economies of Eastern Europe. Still, at the time of writing, Hungary's market system was incomplete and in some respects distorted.
- Hungarians have a much large and a better-quality assortment of goods available to them than do other Eastern Europeans. (Some cynics have suggested that economic conferences and other gatherings of experts and bureaucrats from socialist countries in Budapest tend to be scheduled for December, the better for foreign dignitaries to do their Christmas shopping.)

Despite all these factors, Hungary has never been among the economic pioneers; it cannot even be considered one of the more economically advanced nations. Its per capita gross domestic product (GDP) has been 40 or 60 percent that of Western Europe, and one-third that of the

United States, since the turn of the century. In terms of economic development, Hungary ranks between Spain and Greece, but in those countries there are more significant regional disparities in living standards. In Eastern Europe, the German Democratic Republic (GDR) and Czechoslovakia are more advanced economically, Bulgaria, Romania, and Yugoslavia (which also has a strong regional differentiation) are less developed. Hungary is relatively small: 93,000 square kilometers and approximately 10 million people, roughly about the same as the state of Pennsylvania.

In explaining the Hungary of 1986 to the Westerner, it might help to begin not in the country itself but in the Austrian capital, Vienna—which, at the time of the Austro-Hungarian monarchy, was the seat of the king of Hungary as he was also the emperor of Austria. The city still offers a window on Hungary.

Hungarians do a lot of their shopping in Vienna, not just diplomats and business people, but tourists; of the Eastern European countries, Hungary probably stands second to Yugoslavia in the number of tourists heading West. There are exchange regulations, but every three years, Hungarians may buy a limited amount of convertible currency from the Hungarian National Bank to spend in capitalist countries (and for Hungarians, the exchange of currencies of Comecon [Council for Mutual Economic Assistance] countries is unrestricted). The convertible currency they receive for their forints will allow them about a month in Greek or Spanish campgrounds with modest meals, or two or three weeks in the cheaper hotels of Western Europe's smaller cities. The limits are similar to those France imposed in the early 1980s on the foreign currency that country's citizens could buy for travel outside the country.

Most of the Hungarian tourists swarming west visit neighboring Austria, and those with more distant destinations generally travel via Vienna. Hungarian tourist offices organize countless brief group tours to Vienna—these can be paid for in forints—and they are usually overbooked. The presence of all these Hungarians in the Austrian capital leaves its mark on the city, especially in summer.

In Mariahilfer Strasse or in Kärtner Strasse other visitors to Vienna may overhear conversations in a language that does not resemble English, German, or any of the Latin or Slavic tongues. One may see automobiles, including many unfamiliar small models, with "H" country-designation stickers on them; in shops, there are signs reading *Beszelunk magyarul* ("We speak Hungarian"); and on the streets, sales brochures are distributed in Hungarian. Advertisements declare "10 percent for Hungarians!" or "Cheap accommodations for Hungarians!" or "Hungarian customers may pay in forints!" (True enough, though the forints are accepted at half the official rate of the Hungarian National Bank.) How is it, one might wonder, that so many Hungarians are let out of their country—is it some socialist conspiracy?

Curiosity about Hungary can be partially satisfied by visiting the country itself, which is not difficult. Entrance formalities are minimal: The Hungarian embassy in Vienna will stamp an entry visa in your passport after a short wait, or visitors arriving by automobile or airplane can obtain a visa in a few minutes at the border after a polite customs check. Visitors traveling in Hungary should look at even the mundane sights—the houses and stores—as they will reveal something about the country's social and economic conditions.

Shops and Restaurants

There is competition in providing goods and services. Eyeglasses and watches, for example, are sold and repaired by state, cooperative, and private opticians. There are excellent restaurants—some of them small and privately owned, others owned by the state and leased to the operator (who, as he will readily admit, overbid—putting down, say, 1.6 million forints for three years' rent, an amount he claims will not be easy to recoup). In such places a complete meal, drinks included, costs perhaps 100–150 forints ($1 is worth about 50 forints at the official exchange rate), but one can eat fairly well for only 60–70 forints. There are also exclusive restaurants, some of them in large, state-owned hotels, where a meal may cost 300–500 forints. By way of comparison, the average monthly wage for workers in Hungary is about 6,500 forints.

The large state and cooperative food stories and the small groceries have a wide assortment of goods, but they tend to be crowded in the mornings and late afternoons as both husbands and wives generally work. Hungarians make a lot of trips to the grocery store: Stocking up for a week or more requires a large refrigerator, which most don't have.

Shoes are manufactured by both the public and the private sectors. The state shops have dull names (Shoe Store No. 15) and insipid advertising ("Buy Shoes from the Shoe Store") and sell a product to match. Some of the state products are exported—mainly to the Soviet Union, where Hungarian shoes are considered something special. Private cobblers can make fine shoes to order, but their prices may be three times those charged in the state shops.

Bakeries

Hungarians eat a lot of bread, and the bakeries offer an enormous assortment: potato bread, corn bread, rye bread, soya bread, baguettes, and crescent rolls (butter or salt; small, medium, and large). The plainest bread costs 10 forints (20 cents) a kilo; the more exotic kinds, 20 forints.

Bread is almost always available, though just before a long weekend there may be a shortage or a late shopper may have to make do with two- or three-day-old loaves. Until about 1981, shortages were frequent (even though wheat flour and the other ingredients were in sufficient supply), and the quality was often poor—evidence of the monopoly then held by the state bakeries. Now, with the help of state credits and tax subsidies, about 15 percent of the bread sold in Budapest is produced and marketed by small private bakeries. Loaves from state and private bakeries are displayed side by side in the government grocery stores, and the state product has improved enormously.

Markets

A food market, made up of many small stands, takes up a large part of downtown Budapest. It offers an array of domestically produced goods: vegetables and fruit, eggs, live and slaughtered poultry, dairy products, and sausages from state plants and household abattoirs—nearly everything edible that can be produced in a temperate climate. The market testifies to the fact that the people of Budapest and the other cities in Hungary have not known a serious food shortage since the early 1970s.

The food is sold by state and cooperative shops, private retailers, and the farmers themselves. Prices are usually close to those in the big grocery stores, but shoppers prefer the market if they have the time, largely because of the variety and quality of the goods available there. From a Western point of view, using the official rate of exchange, the prices are very low; if the so-called purchasing power parity rate were used, the prices in dollars would be significantly higher (see discussion in section "Family Budgets" later in this chapter). A kilo (2.2 pounds) of apples in winter costs 25–30 forints (50–60 cents). Chicken costs 100 forints ($2) a kilo; the best sirloin, 150 forints a kilo ($3). A liter of excellent milk, about a quart, costs 10 forints (20 cents) and keeps for about a week.

Hothouse vegetables—lettuce, horseradish, tomatoes—are available almost year-round. The price of such crops out of season, however, is high, partly because, thanks to the scarcity of foreign exchange, few vegetables are imported and partly because greenhouse production is very labor intensive and greenhouses are costly to heat. Another, and very revealing, factor is Budapest's increasingly active "vegetable Mafia," a combatant in a so-called tomato war.

The Housing Market

Although housing supply and demand are in relative balance in the countryside, the urban housing shortage is considered to be Hungary's worst quality-of-life problem, affecting established families as well as young people starting out on their own. Families with a per capita income of less than 3,000 forints ($60) a month are entitled to subsidized apartments, called state flats, after applying to the local council and paying a fee; for a relatively small two-bedroom apartment in an ordinary prefabricated building, the fee comes to 80,000 forints ($1,600).

Priority for these flats goes to families with children, to those living in confined quarters with retired parents or grandparents, and to those who do not live with their extended family but wish to do so. Families who have children, or who promise to have them after moving into a state flat, also benefit from a "sociopolitical discount," which for two children can equal the council fee.

In Budapest, a city of about 2 million residents, some 200,000–250,000 people are eligible for state flats. The wait, however, is often four to ten years, and it has lengthened as the proportion of state flats in new buildings has fallen steadily; in recent years, the figure has not exceeded 15 percent.

The public National Savings Bank builds and sells apartments, giving priority to prospective buyers who can offer a large down payment. Those without much cash can build their own house or buy into a cooperative building in which the flats—each with an additional room in the cellar and a garage—are the residents' personal property. As with other flats and houses purchased outright, property in cooperative buildings can be inherited.

Low-interest loans and other subsidies are available for buying or building flats, under a system designed mainly with sociopolitical considerations in mind. The National Savings Bank offers thirty-five-year loans of 300,000–400,000 forints at very good terms: 3 percent interest, compared to a recent inflation rate of 7–8 percent a year. The bank can also provide a fifteen-year personal loan of another 100,000–150,000 forints, but at 8–10 percent interest. In Budapest, a completed flat can cost 900,000–1 million forints ($18,000–$20,000 in Western terms), including the high, and steadily rising, value of the land.

In addition, state or cooperative companies can use their profits to provide employee housing subsidies of 150,000–200,000 forints, also at favorable terms. Workers in government offices and institutes have similar opportunities, although their employers have less money available for the purpose. All of these subsidies are in addition to the sociopolitical allowance noted earlier: 40,000 forints for one child and 80,000 for two, as well as an allowance for couples who commit themselves to having children later.

The difference between the various credits and the sociopolitical allowance on the one hand and the cost of the flat on the other must be presented to the bank in cash or in the form of a savings account before a construction loan can be approved. This requirement is not necessarily a burden, as the money can be borrowed from friends and relatives and repaid after the credit becomes available. In Budapest and other industrial cities, the great problem frequently is finding land to build on. In these cities, building lots are scarce and extraordinarily expensive; construction workers, building materials, and the required equipment are in similarly short supply. There are small construction entrepreneurs who will build houses on a turnkey basis, but only the wealthy can afford these builders as their charges exceed the unit prices used by the bank in determining the amount of a loan. Young people generally resort to do-it-yourself construction, enlisting the help of friends and occasionally a well-paid expert or two.

In Budapest, do-it-yourself construction can save 200,000–250,000 forints of the usual cost of building a house or an apartment building (prospective flat owners may get together to build their own apartment house), but the task is enormous, and not everyone is up to it. The job soaks up all leisure time for two or three years, during which time rent must still be paid, and the do-it-yourselfer must contend with frequent shortages of materials. Also, for the first few years after any new home is completed, before inflation chips away at the burden, the cost of repaying the various credits is very high. One meets young couples who must devote all of one partner's salary to financing the construction debt—not to mention the cost of furnishing the new home.

The Car Market

One-third to two-fifths of Hungarian families own a car, even though Hungary, which manufactures buses and trucks, produces no automobiles. As a member of Comecon, which encourages specialization and cooperation, Hungary waived car production—not a clever move, in local opinion, as Comecon countries do not produce enough cars to meet the demand and Hungary lacks the hard currency to import Western vehicles.

The model in greatest demand is the Lada, made in the Soviet Union under license from Fiat and locally dubbed the "Fiat Fiatovich." The Skoda from Czechoslovakia, the small and relatively cheap Trabants and Wartburgs from East Germany, the Romanian Dacia, and other Soviet, Polish, and Yugoslav cars are also available. Although new Western cars are not sold locally, some transactions, generally involving barter, may bring in a few hundred Volkswagens or Renaults, which does not make much of a dent in the demand. Of the fair number of Volkswagens, Renaults, Opels, and other Western European–made cars with Hungarian license plates, most have either been imported by Hungarians returning from work abroad or been sent by foreign friends or relatives as gifts, despite high customs duties. These cars may eventually be sold on the secondhand market.

As with new housing, the purchase of a new car involves patience. A 50 percent down payment to the state automobile monopoly earns a place on the new-car waiting list. After a car becomes available—a matter of a few months for the breakdown-prone Dacia, a year or eighteen months for the Skoda, two or three years for the models in greatest demand—the other 50 percent must be paid to take delivery.

Like the prices of other consumer durables and housing, car prices are not unrealistic when converted, at the official rate, into Western currencies, but in terms of local earnings they are very high. The Trabant costs 80,000 forints ($1,600), the 1200-cc. Lada goes for 140,000 forints ($2,800), and the Dacia costs 150,000 ($3,000). The excess demand for new cars determines the prices of secondhand vehicles as well: A one-to-three-year-old car in excellent condition sells for more than it did when new, and even a five-year-old Lada in good condition can cost 90,000–100,000 forints. The shortage also raises the price of secondhand Western cars, which are sought not only for their better quality but for the prestige of ownership. For example, a 1300-cc. Volkswagen Golf, three to four years old and in good condition, can sell for up to 400,000 forints ($8,000). (It should be noted that none of these prices quoted includes the registration charge for secondhand cars, which is 18 percent of the sales price.)

Other Durable Consumer Goods

Most Hungarian households have refrigerators, vacuum cleaners, and washing machines, and it can safely be said that even the poorest have televisions and radios. On the other hand, few Hungarians have dishwashers. Most household appliances are relatively small, and would be considered five or ten years out of date in Western Europe, but their cost is within the reach of middle-income families: 7,000 forints ($140) will buy a good refrigerator with 160 liters of cooling space and a small freezer compartment, and black-and-white television sets are available for 6,000–8,000 forints ($120–160).

Appliances that would not be considered obsolete in Western Europe, however, are rather expensive and available only occasionally. A high-quality, large-screen color television set costs 40,000–50,000 forints

($800–$1000); an older-model color set would cost 20,000–25,000 forints ($400–$500). A stereo, not state-of-the-art but of excellent quality, is in the 40,000–50,000 forint range as well. Small personal computers are available at two and a half to four times the Western European price, according to the official exchange rate. Thus, really up-to-date appliances are bought only by families that are financially well off.

Health Care, Child Care, and Schools

By international standards, Hungary has a high-quality system of health care, with more than 30 physicians and 100 hospital beds per 10,000 people. Treatment—as conspicuously placed signs in hospitals and out-patient clinics note—is available for free. The costs are financed mainly by social-insurance payments, which are set at a specified percentage of wages and paid by the employers.

A peasant or worker whose parents saw a doctor only when it was time to ask for the priest now visits a physician for the slightest complaint. Similarly, people whose parents were on a liquid diet because of a lack of teeth can obtain dentures from the state—though if they don't want their first smile to betray them, they may be fitted by a private dentist at their own expense. Physicians working in hospitals and clinics can also have private practices, but they are liable to a special tax on private income.

Free health care is considered a major achievement of socialism, but many people complain about it; both the pride and the complaints seem justified. The fact that it is free, for example, creates a nearly insatiable demand. Cynics say that lonely old people go to outpatient clinics for the company and that married couples can enjoy a vacation by packing their aging parents off to the hospital. In addition, despite the availability of health care, statistics show that Hungarians are in rather poor physical shape. Many explanations are offered, including alcohol and tobacco use, the sedentary life, and overwork in the form of second and even third jobs. All of these factors result in crowded clinics and hospitals—some of which, moreover, use out-of-date equipment and procedures that were current elsewhere ten or fifteen years ago.

The principle of free care is often subverted by under-the-table fees to physicians—100 forints for house calls, for example, and 200–500 forints to hospital physicians. There is also an established fee schedule for operations and other procedures, such as assisting at childbirth. A person facing major surgery—even in the local hospital—who wants it done speedily, and by a top surgeon, may wind up paying for the privilege. The subject will not be raised explicitly between patient and doctor, but both know the system, and after the operation the doctor will receive

4,000–8,000 forints from the patient or the family. Other health-care workers, such as nurses, are "tipped" less generously; in the hospital, the physician is in command.

There have been many suggestions for doing away with the gratuities. The prevailing opinion is that physicians' salaries should be raised. Currently a beginner earns no more than 4,000–4,500 forints a month, and a doctor with six to eight years of experience is paid about 7,000–8,000 forints. Some people argue, however, that since the fees have become pervasive, even pay increases would not eliminate them. Under another proposal, basic health care would remain free but patients would pay their physicians for other services. Precisely what would be considered basic care, however, has not yet been determined. Still another proposal calls for higher than average social-insurance payments from smokers, drinkers, and the obese.

Women are entitled to six months of maternity leave, and during that time, they receive a state allowance equal to their regular salary. After that leave has ended, one parent or the other is entitled to a leave of absence from work until the child is three years old. The state pays an allowance of 75 percent of the parent's regular salary until the child is a year old; for the next two years, the sum is 1,200 forints a month. Families also receive a supplement of 700 forints monthly after the birth of one child, 1,400 forints after two, and 2,500 forints after three (payable until a child has finished his or her secondary schooling).

Ninety percent of children over the age of three whose parents work attend council or workplace kindergartens, which are usually well-equipped. Nurseries also care for 15 percent of the children under the age of three, an indication that both parents occasionally choose to work even at that stage. Parents must pay for the nursery and kindergarten, though the charges are not burdensome and vary according to income.

Schooling beyond kindergarten, of course, is free. Children attend primary school from age six to fourteen. Classes run from 8 A.M. to 1 P.M., and some students remain until 5 P.M. for lunch, further lessons, and supervised play; for this afternoon care, their parents are charged a small fee. Roughly two out of three children aged six to ten participate in the afternoon sessions. The percentage drops off for older children, as they are better able to function independently.

Education is compulsory until age sixteen or the completion of the eighth form. After leaving primary school, 90 percent of adolescents continue their studies in three-year vocational schools or four-year secondary schools. Ten percent of those aged eighteen to twenty-four prepare for a profession in a university or another institution where, depending on grades and family income, 1,000–1,500-forint scholarships are available. The financial burden is also reduced by the facts that relatively inexpensive meals are available in the school cafeterias and that many of the students live in inexpensive boarding houses.

The institutions of higher education also offer extensive programs for adults, and the number of undergraduates enrolled in evening and correspondence courses is more than half that in the regular sessions. Still, evening and correspondence students don't get as much out of their programs as do those who attend university full-time.

Taxis

A ride from one wealthy neighborhood on the Buda side to downtown Budapest costs 40–50 forints; a ride to the airport, 150–160 plus the customary 10 percent tip. Thanks to the issuance of private taxi licenses starting in the early 1980s—there are also state and cooperative taxis—cabs are in good supply. Some of the private taxis are operated as a full-time business while others are run as a sideline, generally at peak hours, by employees of the state cab companies.

Some of the drivers speak foreign languages and welcome the chance to serve as guides to the city (preferably for foreign currency). Some who have newer Western cars specialize in the tourist trade and charge accordingly. One of these told me he worked for four years at a diplomatic mission in France and bought his diesel Mercedes with his earnings. Returning home, he quit his job to become a private cab driver; on the side, he dabbles in black-market foreign currency. ("You can get caught easily with larger amounts," he noted.) On the black market, convertible currency is bought at a 20–25 percent premium and sold for 35–40 percent above the official rate.

This driver had to do some lengthy computations to calculate his net income. Discounting the five-year amortization on the car, net income from the cab is about 10,000–12,000 forints a month, or almost twice the average salary. To this amount, he adds 2,000–3,000 forints from his currency dealings. There is also a substantial "amortization difference" accruing on his car. The Mercedes could be sold for 800,000–900,000 forints; if he uses it for another five years, he could still get as much as 300,000 forints and buy a new Lada for 150,000. The amortization on the Mercedes, then, plus that 150,000-forint profit, translates into 17,000 forints of extra income each month.

Deducting tax and social-insurance contributions, the driver figured that his net income was in the range of 30,000 forints a month—as much as a minister of state earns. "After five years," he commented, "I'll decide what I'm going to do—continue as a taxi driver with a Lada, start something else, or go back to work in the state sector."

Small Farming as a Second Job

About 20 kilometers from the nearest big city, 15 kilometers from Lake Balaton (a prosperous resort area), there is a village of nearly 2,000 people. The streets are clean, though only the main ones are paved. Trees and flowers abound in yards and along the streets. The houses, for the most part, are small (one story each, with 70–120 square meters of floor space), well-kept, and surrounded by gardens. There are also some ramshackle, deserted dwellings as well as some inhabited houses in poor condition; according to the villagers, these houses were (or are) inhabited by elderly people living alone. There are also some large, attractive two-story houses. These belong to the doctor, the veterinarian, the priest, the chairman of the local agricultural cooperative, and some members of the cooperative who engage in intensive small production for themselves. About one-third of the village's families own cars, generally Trabants or Ladas.

In the center of the main square is a dreadful statue, put up in the 1920s in memory of the people who died in World War I. Next to it is a sort of obelisk with a red star on top and names inscribed in Cyrillic letters; this was erected at the end of the 1940s in memory of Soviet troops who fell nearby. Also in the main square are the church and the primary school, including a basement nursery. Older children attend classes in a larger town nearby or in the city. An office building on the square houses the local council, the local Hungarian Socialist Workers' party organization, and an outpatient clinic.

Nearby, surrounding the square, are the village's restaurant and pub and a store selling a narrow assortment of food, household items, and the like. These small businesses belong to the region's General Consumption and Sales Cooperative. In a newer part of the village are a private car-repair garage—its owner lives in one of the better houses in town—and a private confectionery that sells baked goods and fresh vegetables as well as sweets. For major shopping trips, residents head to the city.

One family in the village consists of a husband (55), a wife (50), and a daughter (28), the last secondary-school teacher in an old town 100 kilometers away. She no longer lives at home but visits often and still uses her old room. The father is a storekeeper at a plant in a larger town nearby. The factory, which produces machine parts, is a division of a state-owned engineering company based in Budapest. The wife is a clerk in a year-round resort that also belongs to a state enterprise. Each spouse has to commute by train for forty minutes to an hour each way—they own a car, but it would be too expensive to use it for getting to and from work.

Their house, passed down through the generations, originally was a cottage with two bedrooms and a kitchen, but additions were built with the help of friends, relatives, and neighbors, and there are now four medium-sized bedrooms as well as a kitchen, an unheated summer kitchen, a large pantry, and a bathroom. The village has no water mains or sewers, but the house has excellent water supplied by an automatic pump from a deep well. Sewage is drained to a tank in the furthest corner of the courtyard, and the tank is cleaned twice a year. In an expanded cellar are tools, barrels, a large freezer, and a coke heater, which supplies both heat and hot water. (A natural-gas pipeline has not yet been constructed to serve the village.) There is no telephone—the entire region suffers from a telephone shortage, and the chances of obtaining one here are almost nil.

There are flowers and ornamental trees in the narrow front yard as well as a large garden of about 1,600 square meters. Behind the house is the couple's small farm consisting of rabbit hutches and a piggery with a self-feeding device, a poultry yard, fruit trees, and a vegetable garden. The husband and wife also rent 5,000 square meters of land on which they grow most of their animal feed, paying the local cooperative farm to do the plowing and other mechanized work. The wife also collects leftover food at the resort, and when there is enough, she takes the car to work and brings the food home for the pigs. The rabbit and pig stocks are obtained from a unit of the cooperative farm, and marketing is done through the cooperative. The couple could choose to be independent of the cooperative, but that would not be profitable.

Workdays are long. The husband and wife get up at 4:30 A.M. to tend to the animals, spend eight hours a day at their regular jobs, and return in the evening to chores on the farm, which also occupy their weekends and holidays. Their major form of entertainment is television, which offers Hungarian, Yugoslav, and Austrian programs. The couple likes to go to movies and the theater in the city but can do so only when their daughter happens to be home or when a neighbor agrees to look after the animals.

The income from their regular jobs comes to about 120,000 forints ($2,400) a year, and their net income from the farm is 120,000–160,000 forints ($2,400–$3,200). A progressive tax is levied on small farms only if there is an income of more than 500,000 forints, so it is not burdensome for this family. Although the couple lives modestly, the farm allows them to eat well and store plenty of good food in the pantry. The house is well-furnished, with a modern television and radio and a small library of about a hundred best-sellers. Numerous houseplants, a few attractive prints and photographs, pictures of the Virgin Mary, and a small statue of Jesus complete the decor. A few years ago the couple helped their daughter buy and furnish a two-room apartment in the town where she works. They paid 500,000 forints ($10,000) down for the apartment, and the daughter raised another 300,000 ($6,000) in long-term credit from the bank. This debt is not a major strain on her finances, as the interest rate is a mere 3 percent; the whole cost to her for the apartment, including maintenance, is 25,000 forints ($500) a year. In addition to her regular teaching salary, she also earns about 110,000 forints ($2,200) a year teaching evening courses.

The husband and wife are gradually reducing the farm's output to supply only their own needs, and they expect to retire in five years—men must be sixty years old, and women fifty-five, to qualify for pensions. How do they see their future? "We have everything we need. Our daughter will get a car, and then it's over," they say. "With the pension and what we have in the bank, we hope we have enough to live on. We hope there will be no war."

Small family farms such as the one just described are a common source of supplementary income. About half the population lives in areas that, while technically part of a city, are essentially rural. Only one-third of the residents of these areas are true peasant families, with members working on large state farms or as part of agricultural cooperatives; the other families rely on more-distant factories and offices for their main income. (There are, of course, families in which, for example, the wife works on a cooperative farm while the husband is a factory worker or a clerk.) It is normal for these rural families to have a small farm producing livestock, fruit, and vegetables as a second source of income.

About 1.5 million families—nearly 40 percent of all Hungarian families—engage in this sort of agriculture, producing not only for themselves but also for the market. Seventy percent of the country's vegetables, 64 percent of its fruit, and 58 percent of its pork come from such farms. About a third of these farms are strictly market-oriented enterprises. In certain areas of production and in the sale of their output the small farms have connections with—and are sometimes fully integrated into—the local large-scale agricultural operations.

Other Second Jobs

Almost all economically active Hungarians—95 percent of them—have a full-time job in a state or cooperative enterprise, a government office, or some other state institution. At the same time, perhaps as many as two-thirds to three-quarters of Hungarian families receive additional income from some other source. A joke, twenty years old but still circulating, illustrates the situation. John Kennedy, Nikita Khrushchev, and János Kádár, the former general secretary of the Hungarian Socialist

Workers' party, are talking. Khrushchev asks Kennedy what the average U.S. worker earns in a month.

"About $400," Kennedy responds.

"And what does he spend it on?" asks Khrushchev.

"Well," explains Kennedy, "between taxes and the rent or the mortgage, he spends $150. He can do whatever he wants with the rest—we don't ask. It's a democracy. What about the Soviet Union?"

"In our country," Khrushchev says, "a skilled worker earns about 180 rubles, and he spends 30 rubles on rent and taxes. He is free to spend the rest on whatever he can get—we don't inquire. We, too, are a democracy."

Kennedy and Khrushchev then put the question to Kádár. The Hungarian responds: "A skilled worker earns about 4,000 forints. He spends 6,000 forints shopping. Where does he get it? We don't ask. Hungary is also a democracy."

Precise statistics on Hungarians' second incomes are lacking. But in addition to small farming, there are other types of second jobs. For instance, carpenters, locksmiths, plumbers, television and radio technicians, and automobile mechanics frequently work for themselves outside of regular hours. This practice is legal, provided a license is issued and a small tax is paid, though most moonlighters don't apply for the license. In the summer, students head for resort areas to work in seasonal restaurants and other businesses (car and boat rental services, for example). Some people work after regular hours or on their days off to build private apartments or do maintenance on them. Still others spend extra hours and weekends at their regular workplace, but not for overtime pay. These workers have been organized into teams to carry out special tasks for an agreed-upon amount of money. Although such teams are often set up by factory managers, some self-selection and self-organization on the workers' part are involved, and the teamwork has elements of private enterprise, although there is no risk and the workers have no capital invested in the "business."

White-collar workers and professionals often have second incomes as well. Office workers, teachers, and engineers living in rural areas usually have their own small farms; factory clerks and engineers may participate in such an in-house "enterprise" as is described above. And more than one engineer works, with or without a license, repairing cars, televisions and radios, or other household appliances.

Professionals may pursue a second job that is more closely related to their field. An architect, for example, may design apartment buildings, private cottages, and vacation homes or may supervise their construction. It is not unusual for an engineer with a large state construction company to work weekends building private houses with the help of a few subordinates from his regular job. On such occasions, the company's equipment may be used—either legally, for a fee, or simply borrowed. Some of the more unusual professional sidelines include small technical-consulting services that work with large companies, small computer-consulting and software-development firms, marriage and legal counseling groups, and travel agencies. All of these organizations are registered with the authorities.

Teachers may instruct classes outside their school or university, and a variety of professionals—researchers and university lecturers, for example—may conduct studies of various kinds. Two of the more unusual of these studies have dealt with soil and water management in the Szeged area and the computerization of the income-tax system. Such studies are also assigned to university departments and research institutes, of course, and the experts working on them (as part of their regular jobs) are well paid.

Second jobs can pay two or three times as much per hour as full-time work for several reasons. For one thing, wage increases in the big socialist enterprises are held down by regulation. For another, even if people need money, they will work at second jobs only if the pay is good. Finally, when people are in business for themselves, organizing their own work, they tend to work harder than they do in the large state-owned plants.

The regular job can be the source of a second income in ways that range from perfectly legal to corrupt. Surprisingly, employees of large companies can earn extra money (from licensing fees, for example) by devising technological innovations. Then there are tips. There is no objection to small gratuities for waiters, cab drivers, service people from the gas or electric utility, or the truck driver who has just dropped off a new refrigerator. People also consider it natural to give a doctor 100–200 forints for making a house call. On the other hand, gratuities to hospital physicians are larger and are considered abusive, as noted above. People resent having to slip money into someone's pocket for surgery, gynecological treatment, or the implant of a prosthesis paid for by the state—but they do so nonetheless.

Shortages offer fertile ground for corruption. Council officials in charge of assigning flats are sometimes caught raking in thousands or tens of thousands of forints. When a Western color television isn't available, a 500-forint bank note will help the store "find" one. If car repairs are delayed because of a missing part, some "gratitude money" to a mechanic who knows a worker at a supply house can help. A private tailor who wants to buy fabric, either wholesale or from the factory, will have to bribe the salesman to reserve what he wants. A small farmer whose produce is bought and exported by a state organization may discover that some money for the official intermediary is more important than the quality of the crop. Most second incomes involve production or service work, but some are simply criminal.

Family Budgets

Family budgets in Hungary, as everywhere, vary widely. But on the basis of conversations with families and people who study them, one can estimate the budgets of two typical families of four: one headed by workers, the other by professionals. In the former, the husband's regular net income is about 7,500 forints a month, and the wife's is 5,000 forints. There is probably about 3,500 forints of secondary income, and because they have two school-age children, they receive a 1,400-forint allowance from the state. Their total income is about 17,400 forints a month.

The family spends 6,500 forints on food, alcohol, cigarettes, cosmetics, and the like and an average of 1,500 forints on clothes. If they live in a state-owned flat or in a home more than ten years old that they built themselves—apartment prices rose 300 percent in one decade—rent or maintenance costs, along with any loan payments, may amount to 1,500–2,000 forints. If the family has a car, operating costs, including insurance, may add 1,500–2,000 forints to the family's expenses (assuming that the car is driven mainly on major shopping excursions and weekend outings). Newspaper subscriptions, telephone—if the family is lucky enough to have one—movies, theater, and other entertainment mean another 1,000 forints. It costs perhaps 500 forints to send the two children to nursery school, kindergarten, or afternoon care. Add 1,000 forints monthly for recurring expenses—trade-union dues, school supplies, income lost because of illness—and expenses total about 14,000 forints, against 17,400 forints of income. In other words, the family clears about 36,000–40,000 forints a year.

The figures are not much different for the professional family although the income is higher. Such families include engineers, economists, lawyers, and others who are not managers. (Managers, of course, earn considerably more than employees, even if the difference is much smaller than in Western Europe and the United States.) The average professional family has a monthly income that is about 2,000 forints higher than that of the workers' family, but expenses are also higher—by 1,000 forints, say, for books, cultural events, and tuition for the children. The yearly disposable income works out to 4,000 forints a month, or about 50,000 forints a year.

Therefore, the income of an average family is about 200,000 or 230,000 forints, and day-to-day expenses come to about 160,000 or 180,000 forints; savings can thus be estimated at 40,000 or 50,000 forints. There are two ways to convert forint amounts into dollars: at the official exchange rate (about 50 forints = $1.00 in 1986) or at so-called purchasing power parity (about 17 forints = $1.00), the latter based on Organization for Economic Cooperation and Development (OECD) and UN calculations in 1985. Among the reasons for the 300 percent difference between the two rates are (1) that the official exchange rate reflects the difficulty Hungary has in exporting to the West and the low prices it receives there (so that it takes lots of forints to earn a dollar) and (2) that many basic necessities in Hungary are subsidized (so that it takes relatively few forints per dollar to find "equivalent" prices). For the purpose of family budget comparisons, purchasing power parity is more meaningful and is used here; for other purposes, elsewhere in the book, the official exchange rate is employed. Thus, in terms of purchasing power parity, the average Hungarian family has an income of $11,700 or $13,500, day-to-day expenses of $9,400 or $10,500 and savings of $2,300 or $3,000. According to these calculations, the Hungarian real value per head of private final consumption was about 30 percent of the U.S. level in 1985 (the latest year for which figures are available).

Day-to-day expenses are not a real problem, provided a family already has a furnished home and a car. The disposable income is even sufficient to buy some new furniture and to take enjoyable, though not luxurious, vacations. The importance of a secondary income is evident, as it provides the disposable part of a family's income.

Problems do arise, however, with regard to the costs of a home, furniture and appliances, and a car. For the professional family, the price of a flat is equivalent to twenty years' disposable income; the down payment required to begin building a flat, five or six years' worth. Buying a small car takes one and a half to two years or more of disposable income (along with two to three years of waiting for a model in great demand). An up-to-date stereo or a color television set takes another one year's worth.

In most cases, therefore, it is an enormous task for young people to set up housekeeping at the start of their careers. Although parents may help out, a young couple may work thirteen or fourteen hours a day and often spend every weekend for two or three years working on a home as well. Of course, some young people do not or cannot take on such a burden, or get no parental help; small wonder if such people feel hopeless or cynical.

Wealth and Poverty

The discussion so far has dealt with average family budgets, but, of course, averages can deceive. There are rich people in Hungary. In Rózsadomb, a neighborhood on the hilly Buda side of Budapest, streets are lined with two- and three-story luxury villas. Some houses have a swimming pool in the yard and a late-model BMW or Mercedes parked in front.

Resort areas—such as the Lake Balaton region or the Danube Loop 40–60 kilometers north of Budapest—are full of vacation cottages, some with rooms for rent. More than one is beautiful enough to be on the French Riviera. On Lake Balaton there are many sailboats and small yachts, some of which are owned by resorts that in turn belong to trade unions or government enterprises or agencies. Other boats are owned by individuals or families.

In villages, one can see beautiful rows of houses with Western cars parked outside. There are some villages in which a successful cooperative farm and the small family farms are nearly merged; in which gas, electricity, and sewage lines have been built at the joint expense of the families and the cooperative farm; and in which personal wealth is seven to eight times, and family income two to two and a half times, higher than the national average.

Who is considered wealthy in Hungary? People with an attractive private house (or perhaps a large state flat in an elegant neighborhood and a vacation villa with several rooms) and a new 1500-cc. Lada come close. So do those who can afford a personal computer for a ten-year old or a car for an eighteen-year old, or who can provide a flat for a child when the time comes. People who can afford to vacation in the Canary Islands, Japan, China, or India at prices that are (from the Hungarian point of view) extravagant are the truly wealthy.

Highly regarded physicians and veterinarians are usually assumed to be rich, thanks to the unofficial fee system. The top managers of large, successful state companies and cooperatives are also considered to be wealthy. People who have worked for several years as diplomats, foreign-trade officials, or officials of international organizations can become well-off.

Many small entrepreneurs are rich, including some who pursue a small business only for a second income. There are also successful fine artists and performers, including pop and rock stars, who have a head for business and are rich as a result. In Budapest one can also find people who have become rich in more dubious ways, as well as some who are corrupt and criminal.

State and party officials are not truly rich. They are well provided for and have a number of perquisites: state cars they may use for private purposes, expensively furnished vacation places at Lake Balaton or in the hills, invitations to join specially organized hunting parties. In terms of personal wealth, however, they take their cue from the top echelon, which includes such puritans as János Kádár, György Lázár, and Károly Grósz. The children of the powerful do have an opportunity to acquire wealth thanks to their good schooling, which includes the chance to learn foreign languages, and their easy access to diplomatic and foreign-trade jobs. As to the number of wealthy Hungarians, some analysts put the figure at 3–5 percent of the population.

There are poor people as well, although their presence is less obvious to the foreigner; poverty tends to be hard to spot in the cities or is concentrated in seldom-visited rural areas. Although one may see disheveled alcoholics (along with some well-dressed ones) on the streets, there are fewer of them than in New York City, Paris, Oslo, or Moscow (at least before Gorbachev's antivodka campaign). Urban slums are unknown or insignificant—there is substandard housing but not on anything like the scale found in other places—and one does not see derelicts sleeping on subway benches in Budapest.

The poor are those people who sleep three or four to a room with a sink on the premises and a toilet at the end of the hall. They can rarely afford to buy meat or new clothes, and from them a doctor who makes a house call refuses the proferred 100 forints.

Retired people on small pensions, whose children help out a little or not at all, figure prominently among the poor. People who retired, for example, ten years ago at age fifty-five or sixty, receive perhaps 60 percent of the real value of their salaries in the form of a pension—enough to manage on from day to day but no more. (Pensions amount to 75–80 percent of a person's average salary in the years preceding retirement, and the purchasing power of the forint is about half what it was in 1976, for instance. About half of the loss from inflation, however, has been made up by the state in various forms to people on small pensions.) These people were not covered by pension plans for much of their working lives, and they receive council aid in the form of cash, often month after month. This additional money helps only a little, and these retirees—generally living in two-room flats in working-class neighborhoods or in small, decaying village houses—simply struggle on, out of sight of foreigners.

There are also an estimated 450,000–500,000 gypsies, of whom perhaps 25 percent have been more or less assimilated: The adults have regular jobs, and the children attend school. Another 50 percent are assumed to be in the process of assimilation, but that is difficult for they must learn a new way of life, one involving fewer children and conventional working habits. The remaining 25 percent live in the traditional manner—essentially, a hand-to-mouth existence with irregular work—and thus, in modern Hungary, in poverty.

The problems of Hungarian gypsies are probably no more amenable to easy solutions than the problems of poor minorities in the United States. The Gypsy Council, an organization that meets regularly in the Parliament building, has acknowledged that the many state-funded initiatives to improve the gypsies' lot have produced some progress, as in housing and education, but that the old dilemma remains: Poverty and backwardness breed more of the same.

2

The Collapse in 1956 and Before (1945–1956)

The Upheaval of 1956

The power structure established in Hungary after 1945, and transformed in 1948 into a one-party system, fell apart at the end of October 1956. The old leaders, Mátyás Rákosi and his followers, were discredited, and their power evaporated. Officials who had been in place for years and who were considered untouchable fled to Moscow. Despair, panic, and vacillation wracked the police and the army. Demands by the opposition within the communist party and by other leftist liberals for radical reforms and for the firing or resignation of old Stalinist leaders developed into street demonstrations and then into the collapse of law and order.

Power was assumed by politicians who had formerly been removed from it. Imre Nagy once again became prime minister (during the summer of 1953, while prime minister for the first time, he had attempted to reform economic policy only to be ousted after a short time and even expelled from the party), and János Kádár became the leader of the communist party. It must be remembered that Kádár was almost a child when he fought the Miklós Horthy regime and that he had risen quickly, while still young, to a leading position in Hungary's illegal communist movement. In the early 1950s, he had been kept in prison for three and a half years, on false charges, by the leaders of his own party.

After demonstrations by hundreds of thousands and the storming of the headquarters of the radio, help was sought from Soviet army units stationed in Hungary in accordance with the Warsaw Pact. Curfew and martial law were announced, with amnesty for those people who surrendered their guns. The appearance of Soviet tanks only added fuel to the fire. The demonstrations became even more forceful, and the armed insurgents put up resistance against the tanks. Two days later, the Soviet troops left Budapest. The ever-changing government, led by Imre Nagy, tried to gain control by turning still-operational units of the armed forces and the organized insurgents into a single paramilitary police force. Workers' councils were spontaneously formed, and they guarded the factories and started to build up their own political organizations. Some of these councils included members of the old management; others were opposed to the old regime.

Of the tragic events that followed one another, I shall mention two. On the third day of mass demonstrations, the demonstrators on the square in front of the Parliament building were shot at, and more than a hundred were left dead or seriously injured. Five days later, the Budapest headquarters of the communist party was stormed: Twenty-five people were killed, and several dozens seriously injured, most of them during the lynching that followed the battle.

The tide began to turn early in November. Some members of Nagy's government, including János Kádár, formed a countergovernment 100 kilometers from Budapest, and despite the protests of Nagy, the Soviet army returned to Budapest to put a stop to the revolt. The next forty-five days were chaotic, with a general strike and isolated street clashes with Soviet troops, with arrests and summary trials resulting in heavy sentences and executions. But an unexpectedly quick consolidation followed: The new regime maintained friendly relations with the Soviet Union and affirmed the hegemony of the reorganized communist party, the Hungarian Socialist Workers' party, while taking note of past mistakes.

The "Hungarian problem," an almost permanent item on the UN agenda between 1956 and 1963, stirs heated discussion to this day, particularly among those people who went through what are often referred to as the "regrettable events" of late 1956. I neither intend to pass political judgment nor wish to analyze the events and the ideologies. I have recalled all these events in order to prepare the ground for the rest of this chapter in which I discuss the economic conditions that lead to the upheaval of 1956. There will, of course, be some mention of political developments as well. In later chapters, I discuss the ways in which Hungarian economic policy changed after 1956.

The Postwar Transformation

Successes in the First Few Years

Hungary—or "Hungary of the lords" as the common people and democratic parties of the time called it—was one of the losers in World War II as the country's cost in lives and property was enormous. About 600,000 Hungarians, roughly 7 percent of the population, died; perhaps half were Jews killed in concentration camps. Including the ravages of the Hungarian fascist troops and the retreating Germans, the war destroyed about 40 percent of the nation's wealth. Homes were ruined, one-third of the bridges were blown up (including all of the bridges over the Danube in Budapest), and 70 percent of the railroad rolling stock was taken out of the country. Ninety percent of Hungary's industrial companies suffered substantial losses, and most of the country's livestock was taken away.[1]

In addition, the truce obliged Hungary—liberated and occupied by Soviet troops—to pay reparations for damage caused as a result of its participation in the occupation of parts of the USSR, Czechoslovakia, and Yugoslavia. Over six years, the reparations amounted to $200 million to the Soviet Union, $70 million to Yugoslavia, and $30 million to Czechoslovakia[2]—a total sum equivalent to about 30 percent of Hungary's annual national income before the war.

Despite the defeat and the payment of reparations, despite the loss of lives in the war and the later starvation, most Hungarians eventually benefited from the postwar social transformations. The real winners were the peasants, particularly the poor and landless ones. After a thousand years, the lands owned by the lords were given to the people who cultivated them.

Before the war, half of Hungary's economically active population had worked in agriculture; the other half had been employed in the industry and service sectors. Three-fourths of the people working in agriculture had not owned land, or had owned a plot too small to support them. It would be justifiable to speak of the country then as one of 3 million beggars—a third of the population. Twenty-two percent of the farmland had belonged to big landowners, with estates of more than 600 hectares; another 23 percent had belonged to other landlords.[3]

Popular commissions were formed in the spring and early summer of 1945 to carry out agrarian reform, on the basis of laws enacted by the Provisional National Government. Estates larger than 600 hectares were entirely expropriated; owners of smaller estates were allowed to keep 110 hectares if they farmed the land themselves, 55 hectares if they did not. The reform affected 35 percent of the country, including 30 percent of the plowed land, 19 percent of the orchards, 13 percent of the vineyards, 32 percent of the meadows and grazing land, and 73 percent of the forests. About 60 percent of the land taken was distributed to individuals; another third, mainly forest or grazing lands, became state or cooperative property.

The commissions gave land to 660,000 claimants and allocated house plots to another 150,000 families, but it was impossible to satisfy all claims. About half of the farm workers, tenant farmers, and owners of

TABLE 2.1
Production of major crops and livestock, 1945–1948

	1945	1946	1947	1948
Crops (as a percentage of the average for 1931–1940)				
Wheat	31	51	52	72
Rye	43	60	69	110
Barley	70	70	64	110
Corn	86	62	82	131
Sugar beets	18	54	120	184
Potatoes	85	57	53	106
Livestock (as a percentage of 1938 figures)				
Cattle	57	59	98	106
Pigs	21	25	53	53
Horses	40	49	71	80
Sheep	20	23	35	36

Source: Donáth (1977), p. 91.

small plots received land; making up 90 percent of the new landowners, they received more than 93 percent of the land distributed to families.[4]

The land reform was a genuine revolution: first because it rearranged the structure of Hungarian society, and second because it was carried out by the people who worked the land. Despite hesitation in some places, the peasants generally accepted the land as their due. And they worked hard once they took possession, often pulling the yoke themselves or turning the land with spades. (Tractors had been practically unknown in prewar Hungary.) By 1948, despite several years of drought, the small farmers were able to produce about as much as the estate-based system had, on average, in the 1930s (see Table 2.1).

In the final year of the war and the first half of 1946, the people suffered from cold and starvation. Unprecedented inflation led to a barter system, with city-dwellers exchanging goods for food, and there was an organized food supply of sorts, mainly in the factories. A voucher system was introduced in the cities, but the vouchers were often impossible to exchange. The stabilization of money on 1 August 1946 made possible a money economy after the harvest. Food became more plentiful in the cities, and people were eating well by 1948.

There were major changes in other areas, but they occurred mainly in two directions. State ownership grew steadily, coming to dominate the economy in 1948–1949; at the same time, central instruments of distribution (emergency measures created during the war and the postwar periods) became more robust instead of reinforcing the market economy.

TABLE 2.2
The degree of state ownership, 1947–1949 (as a percentage of employees)

	July 1947	December 1948	December 1949
Mining	91	91	100
Manufacturing	38	87	100
Transportation	98	98	100
Banking		95	95
Wholesale Trade		75	100
Retail Trade		20	30

(*Source:* Pető and Szakács (1985), p. 103, and Ránki (1963), p. 206.

The first step in state ownership was the takeover of the mines at the end of 1945. The next year, the five largest heavy industry companies (proceeds from which went mainly to pay reparations) and the larger power plants and transmission systems were nationalized. Large banks and the companies they owned were also nationalized in 1947, all companies with more than 100 employees were under state ownership by 1948, and in December 1949, companies with as few as 10 employees were nationalized (see Table 2.2). Under the terms of the truce, companies that had been German-owned became the property of the Soviet Union and were transferred by the Soviet Union to the Hungarian state in 1954. Other foreign-owned companies were also nationalized, partly because of indebtedness arising from their large tax obligations and partly because some of their managers were arrested on charges of sabotage. Those charges, brought against the Hungarian-American Petroleum Company in the autumn of 1948 and the Standard Electrical Company, a British firm, at the end of 1949, had international repercussions.

The importance of nationalization lay not merely in the virtual elimination of capitalist property by the end of the 1940s. The new managers were chosen (and fired) by officials of the communist party, which held a dominant position by the end of that decade, working through state officials. These managers were not expected to make marketing and other business tasks their top priorities; rather, they were to act on the basis of instructions from above.

A series of emergency measures—central distribution of resources, state production directives, and credit and finance controls—were required to rebuild the economy, to restore the transport system, to supply food and fuel to the population, and to pay reparations. As the state's role in the economy increased, formal structures of economic control were gradually established. As early as the beginning of 1946, the communist-controlled General Economic Council, the predecessor of the National Planning Office, was formed to serve as the government's highest economic authority. A system of industrial centers or administrations, organized by sector to control industrial production, was set up in 1948. These agencies owned the companies in their sectors (textiles, for example, or engineering), supervised compliance with production directives, and apportioned investment, supplies, and funds for wages.

Although the agrarian reforms of this period were revolutionary, the situation was somewhat different with regard to the nationalization of the other sectors. That process was revolutionary in the sense that it removed the capitalists' economic power base along with their property, and it did allow the country to plan its economic and political future. (We will see later how the leadership handled the opportunity.) But it was not a true revolution because the nationalization was a planned process, not a response to popular desires.

The people had no objection to the nationalization of the major industries and banks. Such measures were deemed necessary, and they were supported by the workers and the progressive left wing and more or less by the democratic parties as well. However, the nationalization of small and medium-sized businesses was at best supported with reservations. Doubts were raised about whether the new managers— assigned from above or chosen from among the employees—could do better than the old capitalist managers who had worked in the factory themselves, loved by some workers and hated by others but generally respected for their ability. In addition to this emotional aspect, huge problems resulted from the nationalization of these businesses—from their integration into the system of central planning and, later, from their concentration into big enterprises. It is precisely the small and medium-sized businesses that can follow the changes in demand and react to technical progress with small innovations. The nationalization of such businesses has been one of the main factors behind the inflexibility and sluggish performance of the Hungarian economy.

Political Change

Political struggle accompanied—more accurately, created—the economic changes. In the first few years after the war, there was a coalition of democratic parties into the National Independence Front. These parties had cooperated during the war in the so-called Hungarian Front, and they operated now with the permission of the Federal Control Committee, a body representing the Alliles that supervised the provisions of the truce. It was on the basis of consensus among these coalition parties that a Provisional National Assembly, or Parliament, and the Provisional National Government were set up in 1945.

The new government was embroiled in disputes over land reform. The socialist parties wanted to solve the land-distribution problem in favor of the landless peasants and smallholders, the route that was eventually taken. The Independent party of Small Farmers, a long-established group with support from bourgeois elements, was concerned about the middle-class and wealthy farmers. This party argued, with some justification, that giving most of the available land to the landless peasants and small farmers would lead to inefficiency and to shortages of food for the cities and for export.

In the end, however, land reform involved more than party politics (despite such factors as the boost to the Hungarian communist party provided by the Soviet occupation). After the collapse of the "Hungary of the lords," the poor peasants—the agricultural proletarians and semi-proletarians who worked the land—were the dominant social force in changing the thousand-year-old system of land tenure. Nor did power politics determine the course of nationalization, the establishment of central economic control, or the gradual elimination of the market economy. Indeed, the communist party first supported a multiparty, democratic regime and a market economy based on a relatively large state sector and a national economic plan; it expected that there would be a transition to full socialism over the years. The Independent Party of Small Farmers, which won a majority of the votes in the 1945 parliamentary elections, called for a capitalistic market economy, but one that would include a significant state sector and restrictions on monopoly capital.

The communist party's rise to power was aided by its great popular support, especially among the easily organized industrial workers. It became the best-organized political force in the country, with talented leaders and experienced policymakers who had gained experience during years of illegal political work. Most of them had spent the prewar years in Moscow—the party's secretary-general, Mátyás Rákosi, had been sentenced to a long prison term under Miklós Horthy and had been handed over to Soviet officials in 1940—and they had connections with the international workers' movement.

These leaders worked their way to power step by step, putting their own men in key state and military positions without being too particular about the means. In the process, naturally, they could rely on Soviet assistance; Soviet officials, for their part, had great influence in personnel matters (e.g., who should become the interior minister).

The time was one of rising international tension. This was the era of Winston Churchill's March 1946 speech in Fulton, Missouri, proclaiming the need to combat communism; the same year saw U.S. atomic tests on Bikini Island and, for the French, the beginning of their war in Vietnam. Disagreements arose among the Allies over occupied Germany. Germany was divided in January 1947, the Truman Doctrine was declared that March, and the Marshall Plan was announced in June, only to be rejected by the Soviet Union and its allies. The Berlin crisis began in

June 1948; January 1949 saw the birth of Comecon. NATO was created in February 1949; the Warsaw treaty was signed in response in May 1955. Marshal Tito was declared a traitor to the Eastern bloc in June 1949, and the first Soviet atomic bomb was exploded three months later. The People's Republic of China was proclaimed that October; in January 1950 the United Nations recognized Taiwan. The Korean War began in June 1950. World affairs undoubtedly played a part in the communist party's rise in Hungary, but the events being played out in Central and Eastern Europe in turn helped aggravate international tensions.

The merger of the two Hungarian labor parties in the spring of 1948 was a decisive step as it meant that the communist party absorbed and eliminated the Hungarian Social Democratic party, which had played a role in the prewar Parliament and had a solid base in the working class. Tactics that had worked against the leaders of other parties were revived, and communist leaders used slander and false charges of sabotage and treason against both Social Democrats and fellow communists. Many prominent communists were imprisoned, and the former interior minister, Laszlo Rajk, and several other communists who had held high office were executed in 1949. Arpad Szakasits—a former leader of the Social Democrats, president of the republic from 1948, and later head of the Presidential Council—was arrested in 1950. (He was released from prison after five years and rehabilitated.)

Communists were in control not only in Hungary by 1948–1949 but also in the other countries acknowledged at the Yalta Conference as being in the Soviet sphere: Poland, Czechoslovakia, Romania, and Bulgaria. In these countries, too, there were power struggles and trumped-up charges lodged against social-democratic leaders, progressive bourgeois politicians, and some communists.

The Economy in 1948–1949[5]

On average, the national income and the volume of products turned out for consumption in 1948–1949 were equal to or somewhat greater than in 1938. In 1945, manufacturing output had stood at 20–25 percent of postwar levels, increasing to about 33 percent in 1946. Manufacturing output doubled in both 1947 and 1948 so that prewar production was matched in 1948 and exceeded by about 20 percent the following year. This striking growth was made possible by the postwar reconstruction. Power plants were being restored, factories were being rebuilt, and equipment that had been taken out of the country—electric motors, for example—was being replaced. The surplus national income per unit of investment can be very high during periods of reconstruction, and this coefficient was 2.5 in Hungary in 1947–1948, four times its prewar value. In addition, labor was available. There had been 326,000 workers in manufacturing, including mining, in 1938; there were 300,000 in 1946, 350,000 in 1947, and 400,000 in 1949.

The industrial reconstruction was thus a success, particularly when compared with other countries' experiences. Industrial production in Germany and Japan in 1949 amounted to about half of the prewar levels; in Austria, the figure was 90 percent. The Western European countries that had won the war and suffered less damage than Hungary fared little better. At the end of 1949, French and Belgian production was only 20 percent higher than before the war; in the Netherlands, prewar production was exceeded by 30 percent.

Hungary's industrial reconstruction was designed to increase the role of heavy industry. In 1938, the iron and engineering industries represented 23 percent of manufacturing output; in 1949, their share had risen to about 33 percent. In the same years, the food-processing industry's share fell from 29 percent to 17 percent. The rebuilding of the transport system was also rapid. In 1949, 10 percent more railway engines were in service than before the war, and railway performance was far above the prewar level.

Although agricultural production had reached the average level of the 1930s, it was still about 20 percent below the level of 1937–1938, and food supplies were insufficient. The previously landless peasants and small farmers were eating more, and by 1948 a good many peasant families had an adequate diet, which had an effect on the food supply in the cities, though urban starvation was by now a thing of the past.

There was a sharp leveling in consumption and standards of living. The relative and absolute status of skilled workers, especially that of professionals, fell while that of other workers rose. For workers as a whole, real wages were 10–20 percent higher in 1949 than in 1938. Although old and new smallholders, who constituted the majority of the peasants, still consumed far less than industrial workers' families, they were far better off than they had been before the war. The relatively wealthy began to appear on the scene—among them, people in positions of power and speculators who grew rich in times of shortage. The authorities tried, not without abuses, to rein in or imprison the speculators. All in all, the common people were entitled to feel that they were living better and that the future would be better still.

Forced Industrialization

Adopting the Stalinist Model

With nearly the entire economy (except for agriculture and the retail trade) under state ownership by the end of 1949, the development of a socialist system was on the agenda. But what sort of socialism? The role of the newly dominant communist party was crucial and involved questions of how it would use Hungary's economic capacity and where it would lead the restructured society.

There was only one model at the time, and on the whole it was a successful one: Stalin's program of the 1930s, carried out with an iron hand. (The ouster of Yugoslavia from the community of socialist countries and the excommunication of its communist party preceded the creation of the ideology of "autonomous socialism.") To see the Soviet model as something other than simply evil, one must recall the era in which it developed.

By the second half of the 1920s—after the years of revolution and civil war—Russia had completed its reconstruction following World War I. Patterns of ownership were not much different than those in Hungary later: millions of unmechanized small and medium-sized peasant farms; industry, trade, and banking under state ownership; and a restricted market economy. Peasant consumption was far above pre–World War I levels, and less food was available to the urban population. Moreover, the poor urban commodities produced did not interest the peasants very greatly. It became quite obvious in the 1920s that Lenin's expectations would not come true. He had expressed those expectations as follows:

> In one of the most backward capitalist countries the working class has already been victorious. . . . The flow of events forced this country to play *provisionally* [author's emphasis] the role of the pioneer of the socialist revolution, and it has to experience the particularly painful sufferings of the first phase of giving birth. We have every reason to look forward to the future with unyielding conviction, to the future which has new alliances in store for us, and which prepares new victories of the socialist revolution in several more developed countries.[6]

Revolutionary uprisings, in fact, were defeated in various parts of Europe, and the only progress came in a still more backward country, China, after 1925. The capitalist world system was reconsolidating itself during the 1920s, and Stalin was aware of that fact. "As compared with the economically advanced countries," he said, "we are 50 to 100 years behind. This backwardness has to be made good in 10 years. Either we can do it, or we will be crushed to death" (from a speech to a conference of industrial officials, February 1931).[7]

Amid bloody political struggle, including murder, Stalin implemented his ideas in the 1930s. His economic and social policies can be defined as the so-called primitive socialist accumulation of capital and stepped-up industrialization:

1. Abolition of smallholdings through collectivization so that agriculture could be centrally regulated and mechanized and consumption lowered. Sources of accumulation and human resources for forced industrialization would thus be created.
2. The development (mainly with resources extracted from agriculture) of large-scale industry able to produce such things as machine tools, tractors, trucks, and trains in addition to tanks, other weapons, and military aircraft.
3. To achieve this development, an unprecedented centralization of the economic management system.

It was, of course, impossible to make up those 50 to 100 years in a decade. But it is an historical fact that in 10 years, new large-scale industry was giving the Soviet army the weapons it needed to defeat the more highly industrialized Germans.

After the Soviet Union's enormous losses during World War II, reconstruction and further industrialization in that country began under the prewar system of management, and an essentially similar economic strategy was adopted by the smaller countries of Eastern Europe. For one thing, after these countries' social transformation and the creation of spheres of influence, the Soviet example was to be followed as a matter of course. For another, by the end of the 1940s, the Soviet government was not ruling out the possibility of a third world war. This idea spurred the pursuit of communist dominance in the region and the buildup of heavy industry.

It must be noted that in most of these countries the people employed in agriculture made up a very high proportion of the labor force—in Hungary, the proportion was above 50 percent in 1949, close to what it had been before the war. Moreover, as already noted, the agricultural sector mainly consisted of small farms with a productivity that was poor by European standards; there were also landless peasants who did not share in the agrarian reform. It is therefore possible to refer to disguised rural unemployment, and the only way to solve that problem was to increase the number of jobs in industry and services.

The Stalinist model—eliminating the self-regulating market and managing business through central planning—was developed to promote the rapid growth of industry, particularly heavy industry. This was the route Hungary took in the 1950s. The major features of the economic management system adopted in Hungary (and elsewhere in Central and Eastern Europe) in 1949–1950 were as follows:

1. Production and marketing targets were handed down in the form of plan directives, in much the same way that the headquarters of a large, vertically organized enterprise assigns production targets. Higher

authorities decided what and how much an individual enterprise would produce.

2. The central authorities determined the allocation of the resources needed to fulfill the targets, from minutely specified material and work force inputs to investment funds.

3. The processes of production on the one hand and of distribution and selling on the other were separated; specialized monopoly organizations were created for internal distribution and foreign trade.

4. The planning process was a pyramidal one. The central planning agency, the Planning Office, drew up the framework of the plan, taking into account the available resources and capacity; the overall plan also targeted major investments. The Planning Office would then create branch and regional plans—for example, for the ministry in charge of machine production, for the ministry of light industry, or for the local authorities. On the basis of the targets and other data in the plan, these subcenters would create plan directives for the enterprises under their control. At the bottom of the pyramid, the level of the individual enterprise, management and staff were to be concerned only with fulfilling (or perhaps overfulfilling) the yearly plan, though they did try to obtain the easiest goals and the greatest resources possible. Their autonomy was limited to matters of internal administration.

5. The system required an unambiguous hierarchy, with the leadership of the party, the government, and in particular the Planning Office at the top; below, but above the enterprises, were the branch ministries (for example, for metallurgy, light industry, or mining) and the regional and perhaps other intermediate economic authorities. The authorities on this level played the role of owners. They were responsible for the conditions under which the enterprises operated, for choosing managers, and for the assessment and remuneration of the work done (partly by premiums). Production and marketing connections among enterprises were neither direct nor horizontal; customer-supplier relations were organized along the lines of the pyramid of authority and were spelled out in the plan.

6. Commodity and money categories functioned as means by which plan targets could be defined and their fulfillment supervised, not as elements of a self-regulating market. Thus, production output was defined not only by natural indicators but by money value. Plans would assign a certain sum of money for expenses (such as wages) acknowledged as necessary. Enterprises would usually have to cover their expenses from their income—the principle of so-called independent accounting—so the concept of profit entered into the picture to some extent. Prices were set on the basis of acknowledged expenses, and demand-supply relations were acted on only through plans.

7. As workers spent their wages on consumer goods, market mechanisms came into play but in a one-sided way only: Price influenced demand. Demand influenced prices and production only to the extent that the authorities took supply and demand into account in determining prices, investment, and production levels.

This economic management system served the often over-ambitious purpose of "primitive socialist accumulation," the rapid and forced development of heavy industry in the Soviet Union and in the smaller Eastern European countries. One could say that it served well in fostering rapid growth and in creating jobs for unskilled "first-generation" workers, even though the industries in which they worked might have been mass producing out-of-date products. It seems, however, that after the primitive and primary absorption of the resources of extensive growth, this system is not suitable for the mobilization of intensive resources of development.

Hungary's economic and political goals in 1949–1950 were those of Stalinism. Industrialization was to be stepped up as the basis for strategic production. The so-called socialist transformation of agriculture would involve the creation of large, mechanized cooperative farms, and part of the agricultural work force would be transferred to industry. Food for the swollen population of the cities as well as the financial resources of accumulation would be guaranteed by using income drained from agriculture and distributed centrally. According to these considerations, economic ties with capitalist countries would be reduced; forced industrialization would be based on Hungary's own resources, on cooperation with Comecon countries, and mainly on the Soviet Union with its rich raw material resources. These objectives were included in Hungary's first five-year plan.

Full Speed Ahead (Toward Unreachable Targets)

The original version of the first plan, for 1950–1954, was approved in the spring of 1949. A revision enacted at the beginning of 1951 offers a fascinating look at what officials thought could be achieved. The original target for national income was a 63 percent increase over the plan period, or 10 percent growth yearly. The revision called for 130 percent growth, or 18 percent yearly. Similarly, the target for accumulation—net investment plus growth of assets—was doubled in the revision. The share of national income to be budgeted for accumulation was to rise from the 18–20 percent of 1949—a figure that was already artificially high—to 35 percent, of which industry was to receive half. (Even in times of rapid growth, net accumulation is generally no higher than 20–25 percent, and industry's share during periods of industrialization is normally no more than 20–30 percent.)

The overwhelming majority of industrial investment was to benefit heavy industry, particularly mines and metallurgy. According to one slogan, Hungary—short of industrial raw materials, coking coal, and suitable iron ore—would be by the end of the plan period "the country of iron and steel." Industrial growth over the five years had originally been pegged at 86 percent, or 13 percent yearly; the revised plan set the goal at 210 percent, or 26 percent per year. The standard of living was to rise by 35 percent in the original plan and by not less than 50 percent in the revision.[8]

It doesn't take a macroeconomist to see that the figures were extravagant. How did the people who drafted and approved the plan and its revision fail to see that insisting on their fulfillment could produce only economic collapse? The plans incorporated their authors' immense zeal and over-confidence; they also contained gross miscalculations.

Modern economies have a certain more or less constant potential for growth. Depending on time and place, that potential may be 3 percent a year or in an extreme case, 8 percent. Crises such as war or revolution may halt or reverse growth, but when the disruption has passed, the economy will expand at a faster-than-normal rate until it "catches up with itself"—that is, until it reaches the point it would have attained at its normal rate of growth. In economic literature, this stage of accelerated growth is called the reconstruction period. Following this rebound, the economy resumes growth according to the underlying potential.

Figure 2.1 illustrates this point. With yearly growth of 5 percent, national income should increase 1.22 times in four years; in eight years, it should grow 1.48 times. The eighth through eleventh years, however, show a decline due to crisis, a decline that equals four years of normal economic growth. After the crisis, from the eleventh year to the sixteenth year, the economy rises to the level it would have reached without the interruptions. From the sixteenth year on, it grows once again according to its natural potential.

During Hungary's reconstruction period after 1945, growth did accelerate, and the people who drew up the first economic plan assumed that the indicators for 1945–1949 could be extrapolated to the years after 1950. In the end the plan had to fail, and the insistence on fulfilling it shook Hungarian society. Social conflict further hampered the economy, and disagreements within the leadership made matters worse.

The Social and Political Arenas

Throughout the entire first plan period, national income grew by about 32–35 percent (the revised target was 130 percent). Investment roughly doubled, and industrial growth rose by approximately 90 percent (the

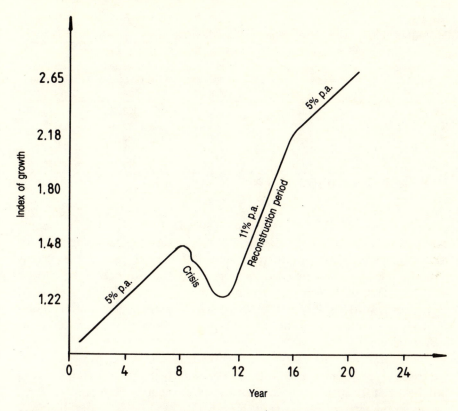

FIGURE 2.1　Trend versus reconstruction: An illustration (*Source:* Correlation established by Ferenc Jánossy [1966]).

revised target was 210 percent). Agricultural production about matched prewar levels by the end of the period, with considerable fluctuations from year to year—it was about 80 percent of prewar levels before the plan went into effect. The data also suggest that real income showed no great leaps either (see Table 2.3).

Thanks to the robust growth of the rate of accumulation, there was a drastic decrease in real wages during three years of the plan period, with a return to about the starting point in the final year. On the other hand, it is not immediately obvious why the real income of working families (strata) was more than 10 percent higher in 1954 than in 1950 (column 3). The answer lies in the fact that women who had previously been full-time housewives took newly created jobs, most of them in industry.

The number of industrial workers rose during the period by about 50 percent, to more than 400,000, even taking into account the decline

TABLE 2.3
Real wages and real income, 1950–1954 (per capita; 1949=100)

	Real Wages in Manufacturing, Blue-collar Workers	Real Income of Blue- and White-collar Workers	Real Income of Blue- and White-collar Strata	Real Value of Peasant Consumption
1950	107	101	103	113
1951	94	90	98	119
1952	85	82	88	106
1953	88	87	91	101
1954	104	102	115	111

Source: Petö and Szakács (1985), pp. 217, 221.

in small industry.[9] Overall, between 1949 and 1955, 1.3 million people entered the labor force. Of these, 700,000 replaced others who had left the work force, so the net increase was 600,000, or 15 percent. About 680,000 were just reaching working age, 120,000 had been unemployed in 1949, 200,000 were former housewives, and 300,000 had been agricultural workers.[10] These figures indicate great social mobility, particularly in the growing number of people moving from farming to industrial work.

From 1950 on, there was a profound transformation in agriculture. In 1949, 2 percent of the working peasants belonged to cooperatives, but between 1950 and 1953, another 23 percent were forced to form or join cooperatives. Harassment, humiliation, and on occasion, blatantly illegal techniques were employed. In addition, the tax burden and the compulsory amount of produce to be delivered imposed on working peasants, particularly the middle-level and wealthier ones (who were often referred to as "kulaks"), were raised to intolerable levels. In 1952, the worst year in this regard, 800,000 peasants were reportedly left without enough grain to make bread or sow a new crop, and 400,000 peasants were sentenced for failing to comply with cultivation and delivery requirements or for hiding their crops.[11] It is hardly strange, then, that many middle-class and well-to-do peasants offered their land, or portions of it, to the state, and from their contributions, state farms were organized. These farms were mechanized but still inefficient.

Parcels of land were joined to create the cooperative and state farms. In more than 20 percent of the villages, peasants who had not joined the local cooperative found all or part of their property taken and other land given to them in compensation. There was little chance to discuss whether the new land was as fertile or as accessible as the old, and the confiscations of course made production even more uncertain.

It was not only the peasants who were harassed; insistence on fulfilling unrealistic industrial plans led to coercion in the factories as well. Piece wages were unrealistically extended, and norm adjustments to those wages were frequently determined and carried out by the central economic authorities. There were efforts to keep workers from changing jobs: The term "left employment deliberately" was introduced on official papers, and penalties—reduced pay, loss of holidays, and the like—were imposed for doing so. These measures provoked resistance, which was punished. Factory engineers lost bonuses or were demoted if the production plan was not fulfilled or the wage bill was exceeded. In more than one case, phony sabotage charges were brought.

Disputes within the leadership were inevitable under such conditions, and party infighting developed. In July 1953, following Stalin's death, a revolt in East Berlin, and initiatives from Moscow aimed at preventing further unrest, Imre Nagy was appointed prime minister—the same position he would again fill in 1956—although Mátyás Rákosi remained in charge of the party. In an address to the Parliament, Nagy announced a program under which economic decision making would respond to reality.

Investment was to be cut, and the investment pattern would be changed in favor of light industry and agriculture. Economic planning would give more weight to the standard of living, coercion and violence against peasants and workers would end, the peasants' tax and delivery burdens would be lifted, and there would be no more conscription into cooperative farms. These measures helped to ease the situation. The peasants' conditions and morale improved, some of the forcibly created cooperatives were disbanded, and the urban food supply grew. Real income had risen considerably by 1954, and the whole country felt relieved. The changes, however, were only temporary.

International tension was still rising, especially with regard to Germany. In October 1954, Italy and the Federal Republic of Germany (FRG) joined the Western European Union, and the FRG was admitted to the North Atlantic Treaty Organization (NATO). In response, in December the Soviet Union jettisoned agreements signed in 1935 and 1941 with France and Britain. The Eisenhower administration committed itself to supporting the Bao Dai regime in South Vietnam. All of these developments affected the situation in Hungary and the rivalries among its leaders. Nagy had not participated in the work of his country's administration since October 1954. In March 1955 he was formally expelled from the Political Committee of the communist party, and in November he was expelled from the party itself. The bullying and violence that had marked the old leadership reappeared. Economic targets once again became unrealistic, the role of heavy industry grew, the standard of living stagnated, and conscription into cooperative farms resumed.

The leadership was clearly unpopular. The already desperate political situation worsened in the autumn of 1954 and later as a number of people who had been sentenced in rigged trials or convicted without any trial, including well-regarded former communists and social democrats, reappeared. It gradually became evident, both to the politically active and to the party's rank and file, that the party leadership was not simply incompetent. It was harming Hungary and discrediting socialism, communism, and the workers' movement. As it turned out, the party leadership was also guilty of fratricide, and the shake-up during the summer of 1956 exposed its conceit and shortsightedness. Rákosi—top man in the party since 1945 and in the government since 1949, a man described in official propaganda as "the father of the Hungarian people" and "the best Hungarian student of Stalin"—was sacked and replaced by Ernö Gerö, the party's second in command, who became first secretary.

The reasons why turmoil was inevitable should be clear: the disintegration of the power structure and the fragmentation of a party whose members were deeply disappointed in their leaders all led to the collapse and upheaval of late 1956.

Pain and Progress

There was more to the Hungarian economy during this period than forced socialization, the setting of unattainable goals, and the resulting strains. Despite all the troubles, national income in 1955–1956 was about 40 percent higher than in 1938. A good part of the increase was absorbed by accumulation, but shortages and queues notwithstanding, the general standard of living rose. The per capita consumption of workers was about 20 percent higher than in 1937—owing mainly, as noted earlier, to the fact that more women were working. Most peasants and agricultural proletarians no longer lived in absolute poverty, despite the harassment they suffered in 1951–1953.

Changes were made in the structure of the economy. The importance of industry, particularly heavy industry, increased against agriculture—too much so, perhaps. In the first half of the 1950s, industrial production rose by nearly 14 percent a year, or by about 70 percent between 1950 and 1955. Employment in industry (including construction and mining) as a share of total employment rose from the prewar figure of 23 percent to 30 percent in 1955. The share of workers employed in agriculture, meanwhile, fell by nearly 10 percentage points, to 43 percent.[12]

The events of the autumn of 1956 must be considered in light of these figures. The workers did not seek a capitalist restoration. Through their councils, they wanted to end the party's despotism and to have factories managed according to their own interests. They wanted a socialist model responsive to Hungarian conditions, not one copied from the Soviet Union. And although they knew that Kádár and some of his allies had served time in Rákosi's prisons (and in Horthy's), they did not easily forgive them for turning to the Soviet Union to solve Hungary's problems.

The 1956 crisis shattered the agricultural cooperatives—two-thirds of them shut down—and in the villages, the wealthier farmers tried to avenge the wrongs done them. Still, the countryside feared a counter-revolution as well. People worried that landlords returning from the West would try to retake their ancestors' lands. The people opposed abuses of power, such as sweeping the farmers' attics clean of grain and coercing them into cooperatives, but they supported the power that had redistributed the land.

It is also worth noting that industrialization has never been achieved without social disruption—one need only recall the England of Charles Dickens's time or the United States at the turn of the century. The most explosive tensions arise when industrialization requires integration into a world market dominated by more advanced countries. In such countries—Greece under the junta, Franco's Spain, Stalin's Soviet Union, or contemporary South Korea and several South American nations—power usually goes to those people who are merciless in acquiring and retaining it. In Hungary after 1945, industrialization was on the agenda.

3

The Decade After the Collapse (1957–1967)

The Fast Consolidation

After the chaos of 1956 there was an unexpectedly quick rebound. The new regime consolidated its power and restored the party's dominance—thanks in part to the quick reorganization and firmness of the armed forces and the judicial system but largely because most people were willing to trust the new leadership. Not only had that leadership decisively overcome its opponents, it publicly disapproved of their methods and promised to improve economic policy and political life. It also pledged that a steady increase in the standard of living would have top priority in economic planning.

Personalities play a part at such times, and the people knew that many people in the party's top echelon had been falsely denounced and convicted by the Rákosi regime. In November and December 1956, while the air in the factories still smelled of gunpowder, the new leaders also showed impressive courage, often visiting factories to calm workers and win their support.

The leadership itself did not expect that the state apparatus and economic system would be repaired so quickly, and another surprise was that damage from the fighting did not keep production from resuming. The workers' councils were to be thankful for another piece of good fortune: The factories had not been looted.

The Warsaw Pact countries, along with China and Yugoslavia, offered Hungary large amounts of emergency credit at favorable terms; almost a third of these credits were raised in convertible currency. As a result, in 1957 Hungary was able to import about 40 percent more than it exported, which increased the value of the products available for domestic use by 7–8 percent.

Early in 1957, the government legalized the higher wages that had been paid during the period of chaos and strikes, thus raising wages at a stroke by 20 percent.[13] Commodity credits, production growth, and curbs on investment guaranteed that this raise translated into a real pay increase. Real wages were 14 percent higher in 1957 than in 1955, and real income per capita was about 40 percent higher than in 1953.[14] As part of the push to raise the standard of living, some of the industrial building capacity that had been idled by the restraints on investment was used to create housing; the number of state-financed homes built in 1957 was nearly twice the 1955 figure.[15] The growth in production created the financial basis for consolidation. There were 5 percent more industrial workers in 1957 than in 1955, agricultural production roughly equalled that of 1955, and the national income was higher. (In 1956, industrial production had been 10 percent less than in 1955, agricultural production 14 percent less, and the national income approximately 12 percent less.)[16]

There were suggestions that the post-1948 economic system be studied with an eye toward radical change, and the administration initiated such a study, involving prominent Hungarian economists, early in 1957. The recovery, however, took place under the established system, and fundamental reform was dropped from the agenda.[17]

Agrarian development policy—a subject affecting nearly half the population in 1956–57—was slated for changes. These will be discussed in detail later, but briefly, the administration was concerned with both the nature and the pace of collectivization. After the land distribution, 46 percent of the country's farms were smaller than three hectares, and 32 percent had three to six hectares.[18] The new leadership envisioned larger farms, suitable for mechanization and efficient cultivation, but it did not pursue this course by impoverishing the majority of peasants, taking their land, and turning a few others into agrarian entrepreneurs. It did not, in other words, choose the capitalist form of concentration. Large cooperative farms were to be created on a voluntary basis.

Moreover, under the agricultural program announced in the summer of 1957, cooperatives were to be formed only when equipment and expertise allowed. Officials hoped that well-equipped cooperatives, producing good yields and wealth for their members, would induce more peasants to join. The process was expected to take ten to fifteen years, but that turned out to be an overestimate—most of the peasantry was absorbed into cooperatives between 1959 and 1961.

The economic system had not been changed, but the cautious pragmatists in power had learned the lessons of 1956. They took as dogma the need for people to feel that life was getting better year after year and took seriously the slogan, "By means of the established instruments of socialism, but better!"

Doing Better Through Plan Directives

The new leadership retained plan directives as the keystone of a planned economy and as protection against the anarchy of the market. At the same time, it admitted the irrationality of having the Planning Office and the ministries make almost all important economic decisions. Under such a system, a host of nonmacroeconomic matters inevitably wind up in the hands of people and organizations that lack relevant information; knowledgeable people at the enterprise level, meanwhile, are subjected to rigorous control by the state and party bureaucracies.

The plan directives were simplified according the theory that factories did not need to be told in minute detail what and how much to produce. Instead, the value of the output would be specified, with quantity targets handed down for only a few major products—for example, coal, electric power, some foundry products, or meat—for which central distribution was considered necessary. For these products, the Planning Office would draw up production and distribution plans. For exports, only the forint value of the goods to be delivered to the foreign-trading company would be specified; both the trading company and the manufacturer would have an interest in obtaining the largest possible amount of convertible currency for the product. The plan directives for raw materials would be based, not on quantities, but on specified forint limits that could be spent on them. Most investment decisions would still be centralized, but enterprises would be allowed more initiative, for example, in making small investments or using their own funds to update their equipment.

The abolition of the compulsory delivery system—the agricultural equivalent of production quotas—was another important step. Under the previous system, peasant farmers, including those on cooperative farms, had been told, on the basis of regional and community plans, how much wheat or corn or how many fattened pigs they would have to sell to the state retailers—at prices well below the cost of inputs. Now, most agricultural production would be determined by contracts between the state purchasing monopolies and the cooperative farms, and free marketing of farm products would be permitted.

A more realistic price system was introduced in 1959. Prices set by the Price Office (or for less important products by the appropriate ministry) would now be based on the generally acknowledged input costs and a profit of a few percent. The new system put an end to the practice of setting prices, particularly for raw materials, that were well below the input costs. As a result, the producer prices of coal and large-scale electric power trebled, those of other raw materials doubled, and the prices of wheat and other crops—sugar and carrots, for example—went up by 150 percent.[19] Consumer prices were not raised substantially, however, because of the very real fear that such a change would mean a sharp cut in real income for a large part of the population. The differences between consumer prices and the new producer prices were bridged by minutely specified turnover taxes and commodity price subsidies.

The central control of wages down to the individual level through norm specifications and centrally controlled norm corrections was discarded. Enterprises were told what their workers' average wage should be, and a ceiling was placed on their wage budget, but they were otherwise free to determine pay levels and the forms and terms of wage payments. The size of a factory's wage budget usually hinged on its success in fulfilling the production plan; each 1 percent deviation from the output target would change the wage bill by, say, 0.3 percent.

Under the new regulations, profit had a place in the planned economy as enterprises received a share of their profits—or, more accurately, of their annual increase in profits. With prices fixed by the government and more or less unchanged product lines, this arrangement gave factories an incentive to cut costs. Part of their share of the profits was to be invested in the plant or equipment at the managers' discretion; the remainder of the profit share served as a bonus fund. The system was intended to inspire rational management, a reasonable use of resources, and profitability—always, of course, within the boundaries of the plan directives.

Industries were reorganized in the first half of the 1960s. Factories were merged, and the large vertical enterprise, a structure that still exists, came into being. The average number of workers in state industrial companies rose from 639 in 1960 to 1,335 in 1965, but enterprises with no more than 1,000 workers employed 42 percent of the state industrial work force in 1960 and only 18 percent in 1965;[20] in advanced capitalist countries, the figure is generally 40–70 percent of the industrial work force. The new industrial enterprises had an average of 4–5 factories apiece as opposed to 1.1–1.4 in the advanced capitalist countries.[21]

The rationale for merging factories was that reducing the number of enterprises would give central planners more time to concentrate on major problems. Enormous amounts of work and red tape were involved in allocating production targets and resources, and larger enterprises could easily handle minor changes, which would eliminate the need to amend the overall plan. Larger enterprises also lent themselves better to input and output quotas specified mainly in forints and could deal more effectively with suppliers and customers. Research and development departments could be formed to help enterprises pinpoint their investments to improve technology and to eliminate bottlenecks.

Other socialist countries have attempted to refine their planning systems. The Soviet Union's so-called Kosygin reforms of the mid-1960s resembled the Hungarian program in several respects, but those reforms were introduced only as an experiment and were eventually blocked. The ideas discussed at that time resurfaced, however, in the call for reform issued by the USSR's February 1986 party congress.

Although the logic behind Hungary's changes seems apparent, the changes did not—and could not—fix the fundamental flaws in the country's economic system. The creation of giant enterprises did make the economy more flexible, but it did not lead to basic changes in the relationship between enterprises and the central economic authorities. The large enterprises behaved as their predecessors had, taking the path of least resistance in production and lobbying for bigger budgets. The big enterprises found their hand strengthened in the planning process, because since they represented entire industries, or large portions of industries, they were in a position to insist more strongly on their demands. If they were not given the investment funds, raw materials, import quotas, or wage increases they sought, they could threaten stagnating production, shortages in the domestic market, and shortfalls in export production. Decentralized decision making also meant that bargaining between an enterprise's headquarters and its subunits to some extent simply replaced bargaining between the enterprise and the central planners.

The new producer prices were sounder than the old ones, which had been untenable without state subsidies, especially for raw materials, but they were no panacea. Even if the new prices accurately reflected costs at the time of the 1959 price adjustments, they still did not reflect supply and demand, as this was not the pricing system's goal and could not be in the absence of a functioning market. In any case, the 1959 prices were out of date in a year or two, because of changes in production and technology, but continuous price revisions would have made it impossible to adhere to the plan. The share of prices earmarked for profit was therefore differentiated more and more each year. This situation gave enterprises an incentive to stress the production of certain goods and to neglect others, regardless of demand. Accordingly, the people drawing up the plan directives had to increase the number of products for which production and distribution targets were specified in physical units or units of measurement, thus reducing the simplification of the overall plan.

The principle that enterprises should receive a fixed share of their profit increases also led to problems. Enterprise A, expected to achieve a large profit increase, might fall short, but it could still receive more in profit sharing than enterprise B, acknowledged in the plan as having less potential but nevertheless exceeding its target. The share system soon had to be adjusted to take fulfillment of the profit plan into account.

The main features of the wage system introduced after 1957 have been preserved. With an overheated labor market, and without really profit-oriented enterprises, Hungary has been unable to dispense with that system even though the plan-directive system has been abolished. The new purchasing and pricing systems in agriculture incorporated market elements, so that prices, and thus producers, responded to some extent to supply and demand. It must be added, however that after the collectivization of agriculture, prices lost much of their significance.

The Collectivization of Agriculture

The agricultural program adopted in mid-1957 was discarded after a year and a half, and the final push toward collectivization began in 1959, years earlier than expected, because the administration decided to speed up the formation of cooperatives. There were several reasons for this change. Bulgaria's farms had been collectivized by the autumn of 1958, and large-scale farms occupied 75 percent of Czechoslovakia's agricultural land and 55 percent of Romania's.[22] Seeing that a similar process at home was inevitable, Hungarian peasants stopped investing in their farms. Also, the leadership had room to maneuver, thanks to the speed with which it legitimized its power. Large investments would be needed to collectivize agriculture, but the leaders knew that industrialization and sectoral shifts would force changes in farming. In 1958, more than 40 percent of Hungary's economically active population still worked in agriculture, and in a socialist system, nothing but collectivization could guarantee that this share would fall while production rose.

The agricultural cooperatives were formed in the winters from 1958 to 1961, and at the end of that time, 94 percent of Hungary's farm workers belonged to cooperatives. Recruiting was less coercieve than it had been—the peasants were not forced to join by dint of economic ruin—and this time, there was no declaration of rural class struggle. Under Rákosi, the slogan had been, He who is not with us is against us. Kádár turned it around: Whoever is not against us is with us.

There was a special effort to persuade respected middle-class farmers to join the local cooperatives since once they signed up, the rest of a village would generally follow. The members of such cooperatives decided for themselves whether to admit wealthy peasants or kulaks, the rural bourgeoisie, who regularly employed others on their farms. Villages were to be collectivized as a whole, which meant there was no need to apportion land; large tracts could be put together in less time with less conflict. The creation of separate cooperatives in some villages by middle-class peasants was not prevented. In contrast to the old system, the peasants usually elected the cooperatives' leaders.

The benefits of membership in a cooperative—pensions and health insurance—were particularly important to older peasants. In addition, cooperatives enjoyed several important state subsidies, and during the years of collectivization, nearly half of the income paid out by the cooperatives to their members was reportedly financed by the state.[23] Cooperatives were also required by law to pay rent on land that they used but which remained the property of a peasant.

There were still too many cooperatives for the available equipment and know-how, especially because private production did not die out. Peasants—particularly former smallholders—chafed under the disorganization of the cooperative farms. Faced with this problem, the authorities tended to look the other way if peasants farmed small household plots and raised their own animals. So-called family-share farming was also permitted. Under this system, part of a cooperative's land—a few acres of corn, for example—would be assigned to a particular family as its main responsibility, and the family would then be entitled to a certain amount of the crop.

To dogmatists, this private production had more to do with "peasant greed" than with collectivization. The government, to its credit, was more pragmatic, first tolerating and then legalizing family-share and household-plot farming. The importance of family-share cultivation is clear from the fact that in 1966, it absorbed fully one-third of the time put in on cooperative farms to raise hoed plants. As for the cooperatives' household plots, the income they produced in the first half of the 1960s (including food grown for the family's own consumption) was higher than the income from the cooperatives.[24]

The shortage of mechanization and expertise remained a source of considerable frustration throughout the 1960s. But thanks to the spread of household-plot and family-share farming, if life in the villages was still far from idyllic, it was at least calm; likewise, the cities' food supply, while not plentiful, was adequate. The 1970s saw the integration of large-scale and household-plot production, and it is worth noting that in 1980, China began to introduce similar methods to increase that country's production. There are clear similarities between the responsibility system introduced in Chinese agriculture in the 1980s and the family-share and household-plot systems in use in Hungary.

The Risks of Economic Policy

Inconsistency was typical of the policy toward economic development, allocation of resources, the industrial structure, and the standard of living. On the one hand, the government knew that the centralization of economic decision making required that it be very attentive to actual

TABLE 3.1
Hungary's three-year plan, 1958–1960 (1957=100)

	Planned	Actual
National Income	114	125
Industrial Output	122	139

Source: Bauer (1981), p. 114.

TABLE 3.2
Accumulation, 1958–1960 (as percentage of national income)

		Of Total, Growth of	
	Total	Fixed Assets	Stocks
1958	17.5	13.6	3.9
1959	20.2	14.9	5.3
1960	25.6	18.6	7.0

Source: Bauer (1981), p. 119.

conditions. It knew that a system based on plan directives runs a constant risk of overheated growth, which could lead to imbalances, swelling accumulation, and finally, crippling shortages. (That such things could be said, incidentally, was evidence of an increasingly liberal attitude toward research and publication. In 1966, the party acknowledged what was already established practice, declaring that no topic or thesis was taboo in scientific research, although reasonable self-censorship was expected in works intended for the general public, and it paid attention to the resulting publications.)

On the other hand, it was hard to resist the temptation to accelerate development. The advanced capitalist economies were growing rapidly, stumbling over minor recessions at worst, and their standards of living were on the rise. The socialist countries had to develop quickly if they were to overcome their historic disadvantage. In early 1959, Khrushchev and the Twenty-First Congress of the Soviet Communist party announced a program of catching up with the most advanced Western economies. Ambitious economic plans followed in each of the socialist countries— plans that were eventually to prove more or less unrealistic.

As Table 3.1 indicates, Hungary's 1958–1960 plan did not take into account the leadership's quick consolidation of power, which gave the economy a major push. The figures for accumulation are given even more revealing (see Table 3.2), as they show that the government was unable or unwilling to hold back the investment surge. The amounts budgeted for investment were rising—by 34 percent in 1959 and 11 percent in 1960. Investment was overheating, and in 1961 steps were taken to cool it down. The administration cut investment by 5 percent over 1960,

TABLE 3.3
Estimates of annual growth, 1959 and 1961 (in percent)

	Published in 1959	Published in 1961
National Income	6.0	6.5–7.0
Industrial Output	7.5–8.0	9.0–9.5

Source: Computed from Pető and Szakács (1985), p. 394.

partly by halting investment projects and partly by scrutinizing new projects much more carefully. The changes in estimated growth rates for the 1961–1965 plan period also show the economic acceleration (see Table 3.3).

Between 1960 and 1964, national income rose by 5.5 percent annually, industrial output by 9 percent. After the containment of 1961, investment rose by 15 percent in 1962, 13 percent in 1963, and 5 percent in 1964—in all, by nearly 40 percent in three years. A new slowdown had to follow, and in 1965 investment remained at its 1964 level, national income held steady, and industrial output rose by 4.5 percent.[25]

There were many reasons to restrain investment. The number of buildings under construction and the backlog of investment projects were skyrocketing, and construction and industrial-engineering capacities could not keep pace. Still, public consumption, real wages, and real income were rising (real wages stagnated only in 1965) and the government dared not do anything that might cut the standard of living. The result was a plunge in the foreign-trade balance, from a surplus of 600 million foreign-trade forints in 1958 to a 1.2-billion deficit in 1960, a surplus of 20 million in 1961, and a 1.7-billion deficit in 1964.[26] Domestic consumption was 0.1 percent higher than national income in 1961 and 3.3 percent higher in 1964.[27] Finally, the government put on the brakes.

The tension between zeal and pragmatism was also apparent in the way investment funds were channeled. Transportation's share doubled between the 1950s and the late 1960s: The road and rail networks desperately needed rebuilding, and with the large enterprises shipping goods from one factory to another, demand for transport was growing faster than the overall economy. Agriculture's share of investment grew sharply as well, from not much more than 10 percent in the early 1950s and 1958 to 19 percent in 1964 and more than 20 percent later on. Nearly 60 percent of the agricultural investment between 1950 and 1970—largely in the form of state credits, later repaid—went to replace land taken out of cultivation in order to provide industrial sites, to reduce the farm labor force, and to provide the fixed assets needed for large-scale production.[28] After the proper equipment became available, large farms became the norm from the late 1960s on.

These investment shifts were possible because industry's share, more than 40 percent, was kept relatively steady, and the 30 percent-plus share for commercial and communal purposes was cut by 6–7 percentage points. But the balancing act caused problems. Investment in communications, hospitals, schools, housing, cultural institutions, and the like languished, which created immediate hardships and risked bottlenecks later on.

According to official intentions, industrial development was to concentrate on those industries in which Hungary was traditionally strong, in which domestic know-how was available, and for which the raw-material and energy requirements were minimal. In the late 1950s and early 1960s, the areas chosen for special attention included the power industry (for example, the productions of transformers), telecommunications, the production of diesel engines and ball bearings, and precision engineering. Some of these development efforts did not always pan out, however, and moreover, other industrial branches clamored, often successfully, for their part in development and investment. So reasonable intentions were often not crowned with success. The economy was simply not set up to let efficiency govern the rise and fall of industries, and—as is discussed later—Comecon relations were also not favorable to these intentions.

Successes and Failures

In the decade after 1957, Hungary's national income rose by 75 percent, or 5.5–6 percent annually. Industrial output rose 230 percent, or 8.5 percent per year. Agricultural value added held steady while agricultural output rose by 25 percent. From 1950 to 1967, the national income rose 250 percent, industrial output 400 percent, and agricultural production nearly 150 percent.

The standard of living also rose considerably. In the ten years leading up to 1967, the real wage per employee increased 130 percent, or 2.6 percent annually. Because of the growing number of wage earners, workers' real income more than doubled from 1950 to 1967. Real peasant consumption per capita rose 35 percent in the ten years after 1957 to 180 percent of the 1950 value.[29] By international standards, these figures were neither insignificant nor extraordinary. In 1937, Hungary's per capita national income had been somewhat below average for the less-developed southern European countries, such as Greece, Portugal, and Spain; in 1965, Hungary surpassed them.[30]

The rise in the employment rate, however, was a major achievement. It rose steeply between 1949 and 1967, especially among women, and Hungary achieved full employment by the second half of the 1960s. This was one of the basic agents of development and, typically, a sign and

TABLE 3.4
Distribution of workers by sector, 1941–1965 (in percent)

	1941	1949	1960	1965
Agriculture	51	52	37	30
Industry	20	19	28	34
Construction	2	2	6	6
Services	27	27	29	30

Source: Timár (1981), pp. 82, 92, 103.

measure of extensive development. Employment patterns, meanwhile, were changing greatly, as is shown in Table 3.4.

From 1949 to 1965, the number of agricultural workers fell by 800,000, or nearly 40 percent. The number of industrial workers grew by the same number, almost doubling in the process. At the same time, Hungary's industrial structure, like that of other countries, was changing. The engineering and chemical industries were assuming a greater role, in terms of both volume of production and size of work force, while mining and textiles were becoming less important. Leading the way were telecommunications, vacuum engineering, precision engineering, and pharmaceuticals[31]—fields that stressed know-how more than raw materials. The production of chemical fertilizers also grew dramatically, and several major petrochemical projects, chiefly involving plastics, were begun in 1962–1963. In short, Hungary was establishing the framework of a modern industrial economy.

Still, no real content filled that framework, and the economy suffered from many handicaps.[32] Technical standards were still low in industry that was initiated by the state and developed quickly with money from the state. Foreign trade, important to a country with a small domestic market, also posed problems. Although one-third of Hungary's trade was with members of the Organization for Economic Cooperation and Development, its exports to those countries consisted mainly of food and semifinished industrial products of mediocre quality. Of Hungary's imports from OECD members, only 10 percent was capital equipment.

Sixty percent of Hungary's trade was with Comecon countries, and in the short run this trade worked to Hungary's advantage. Primary energy supplies (oil and coal) and raw materials—55 percent of Hungary's Comecon imports and 70 percent of its imports from the Soviet Union—were guaranteed under long-term agreements, even if shipments were often too small or late in arriving. But the prices used were simple clearing prices, and did not express any real international standard of value. The growth of Comecon trade, and of the industries that produced for it, did little to spur efficiency.

Mass-produced goods, exported under agreements between state authorities, made up 60 percent of Hungary's shipments to Comecon countries. Hungarian enterprises were required by plan directives to supply the goods, enterprises abroad were obliged to accept them, and the resulting quality can be imagined.[33] A decade later, when Comecon markets grew tighter and Hungary set its sights on the advanced industrial countries, particularly in Western Europe, it turned out that the country's rapidly developed industries offered little in the way of export opportunities.

The problems inherent in the Stalinist model became clearer and clearer in the later stages of industrialization, and by the second half of the 1960s, the system of economic management was itself Hungary's worst economic problem. At the risk of repetition, the weaknesses of such a system can be summarized as follows:

1. The structure of the planning system encourages each level of the pyramid to acquire large amounts of concealed reserves. At the lowest level, the enterprise seeks the easiest possible targets and plenty of resources to achieve them. Its supervising authority, while demanding that the enterprise make more "realistic" plans, has much the same interests. Such forces burden the planning system (both vertically and in relations among enterprises) with the well-known "plan bargain."

2. Market mechanisms work in isolated cases at best. Therefore, there are practically no precise measures of the enterprises' activities, and there is that much less pressure to be rational in current business activity and in planning. Laws and regulations are intended to substitute for the market.

3. Some special authorities and regional agencies naturally favor their own jurisdictions, seeking the greatest amount of resources for the enterprises under them. To win these resources, however, they rely not on raising profitability but on building and maintaining good relations with their bosses. The resulting status-based system hampers the economy.

4. Chronic shortages result. As János Kornai puts it, such shortages are not caused by the producer's natural desire to expand but from the fact that this ambition does not run up against realistic barriers. In Kornai's terms, the budget constraint is "soft."[34] The conflict between the enterprises' aspirations and demands on the one hand and available resources on the other must be settled by the highest macroeconomic authorities. At that level it is hard to reconcile the conflicting demands, particularly because detailed economic knowledge is lacking and the information that accompanies the requests is usually biased. In addition, high-level decisions take political as well as economic considerations into account.

5. As a consequence, efficiency is low compared to the development level of the production forces. Sources of intensive growth, a socioeconomic climate propitious for human creativity, are not free to develop.

6. In the corporate structure of the economy the multiplant, horizontal firms prevail. Monopolies thus arise, and they burden economic relations and contribute to the hesitations of central selection as large firms are generally more successful in bargaining with the authorities. On the other hand, small and medium-sized firms are largely absent, even when one includes the producers who specialize in subsidiary activities (the so-called production and service background). This factor leads to the impoverishment of cooperation, compels large firms to be more autocratic, and thereby contributes to an economy that is oriented toward modest mass production, has a rigid structure, and lacks innovation.

7. There is almost no inducement for firm specialists to follow market events and to react to them, in order to seek an optimal combination of production factors. This situation is the result of having centrally determined production targets and from the fact that production and sales are organizationally separated. Under such circumstances people with good personal contacts to the bureaucracy, not innovative people, are chosen for managerial posts.

In Hungary, as in other socialist countries, these problems have become increasingly obvious. It has also been recognized that given the economy's established framework and the resources, efforts must focus on updating production techniques and products, taking advantage of the international division of labor, working daily to develop and grasp sales opportunities, and making production and marketing more flexible. The industries and factories that cannot adjust will lose out. However, such policies cannot be carried out under highly centralized planning; the economic system cannot interfere with an enterprise's autonomy or rational management. In other words, radical economic reform—moving beyond the Stalinist system—has been placed on the agenda.

4

Reform: The First Years
(1968–1972)

Antecedents

Visions of Communism

According to the comparative-economics textbooks used in U.S. universities and many political-economy textbooks published in the socialist countries, socialism, proceeding according to a social plan, and the self-regulating market are generally considered to be irreconcilable; indeed, the market is considered a peripheral element at most in the socialist economy. To understand this approach, one must look at Marx's thinking.

Marx based his analysis of nineteenth-century capitalism on the idea that a communist society was inevitable. Along with Engels, he believed that capitalism in the advanced countries would be overthrown in the near future; at the same time, he expected a long, difficult transition between the collapse of capitalism and the advent of communism. He termed this transition the "primitive communist society," the first phase of communism to emerge from the capitalist establishment. Most people would still work in order to survive; the inequality of distribution according to work, rather than according to need, would persist.

Believing that the details could not be worked out in advance, Marx and Engels provided only the most general outline of life under communism. Only the pressure of debate, in fact, prompted them to set down a few concrete ideas about the transitional state.[35] Still, Marx and Engels (and their followers) clearly assumed that following capitalism's demise, an economy would arise in which there would be no commodity relations, in which the distribution of labor and means of production would be organized directly by society rather than through the market. They had in mind distribution by means of "work receipts," with consumer goods being distributed according to work performed. Accordingly, they supposed that a short time after the overthrow of capitalism, money and other commodity categories would cease to exist.

The keystone of Marx's and Engels's thinking was their philosophy of history, which appears clearly even in their early writings. In primitive society, they believed, economic (production) relations were clear. Everyone knew his own, and everyone else's, role in the division of labor, and everyone shared in the fruits of collective labor. Later on, thanks to the increasingly complex division of labor and the rise of private ownership, economic relations were no longer so direct and accessible. Instead, they took the form of commodity relations, filtered through the market.

According to this line of thinking, capitalism is the highest form of indirect economic relations. Under it, not only are products commodities, so are the factors of production: land, capital, and—above all—human resources. Economic development accelerates dramatically under such conditions, and in the process, economic activities take on a social dimension. They outgrow local markets and even national boundaries. Marxist theory holds that private ownership and the social aspects of economic activity are contradictory, with the conflict expressing itself in unemployment and recurring crises. Society can master the contradiction only by abolishing private ownership of the means of production. When this task has been accomplished, economic relations will once again become tangible and accessible for the participants, and commodity relations will cease to exist.

Marx found that under capitalism, increases in productivity and wealth did little to relieve workers' poverty; that after a certain point, capitalism, carrying the enormous weight of unemployment, stumbled from crisis to crisis. One could say that he recognized the forces that led to the depression of the 1930s, but he did not see that even under a system of private property and capitalism, workers' consumption could grow at roughly the same rate as productivity. Nor did he foresee that with Keynesianism and the New Deal, the state would become an active participant in the market economy and, more or less, control its cycles.

The Marxian wing of the international labor movement held that in the economic formation succeeding capitalism, people would live according to directly organized economic relations; i.e., after a victorious socialist revolution, commodity production, money, and the market would soon cease to exist. After the collapse of czarist Russia, Lenin and his circle took power in an underdeveloped country bled white by three and a half years of war; the economy was destroyed, there was starvation in the cities, and the revolutionary army soon found itself fighting a civil war. An austere, naturalized economy, referred to as war communism, was put in place as a result. The peasants, who received land as a result of agrarian reforms, had to hand over their entire surplus. Most of the nationalized factories produced directly for the army. Workers and civil servants received their rations of food, tobacco, and—rarely—manufactured goods such as clothing at their workplaces.

The country's leaders knew that war communism was a response to an emergency, but they also considered it the first step toward socialism. The population accepted the naturalized economy—or had to accept it—in the midst of civil war, but later on, starvation and spontaneous uprisings showed that such an economy was untenable. Peasants had little interest in producing a surplus and hid what they did produce; workers picked up their rations and slacked off on the job. The leadership realized that without the reintroduction of some form of commodity production, there would be a political and economic collapse.

As a result, the New Economic Policy, (NEP) was introduced in 1921. Taxation of agricultural produce replaced the compulsory delivery of surplus; the remaining produce was acknowledged as the peasants' property and could be sold. An exchange of goods between town (industry) and village (smallholder farms) was organized, and the scope of money and commodity categories—price, money, credit, cost, profit, etc.—was gradually broadened.[36] The new policy was a success. With the limited revival of commodity production, output and trade picked up, living standards improved year by year, and reconstruction was achieved in five or six years.

The NEP can be interpreted in two ways. From one point of view it was a retreat, albeit a necessary one to establish socialism in a poor country in which state-owned industry, banking, and the like had to operate in an economy dominated by small peasant farms; the retreat was to end with the organization of large-scale agriculture. This viewpoint conforms to the Stalinist model: a naturalized economy in which the market does not function (or more precisely, functions only in the market for consumer goods and there only partially) and in which money and commodity categories discharge the function of records and control. From the other point of view, the NEP demonstrated that socialism involves commodity production and commodity relations.

Reform Movements in Eastern Europe: Two Versions

Hungary has not had a monopoly on the problems of running a socialist economy, nor on efforts to solve them. In the first half of the 1960s, the problems were becoming more and more apparent in nearly every Comecon country, including the Soviet Union. Government officials as well as economists acknowledged that the fault lay in the economic system itself, not in specific decisions or human error.

The investment intensity of economic growth—the amount of investment needed to raise national income by a given measure—was increasing steadily in the Comecon countries. Shortages became more acute, not only of consumer goods but of raw materials, semifinished products, and capital goods, while stocks of hard-to-sell goods mounted. The plan directives could not accommodate rapid changes in public and industrial consumption. The growing inventories of unsold goods also contributed to the growing rate of accumulation; as a result, the growth rate of public consumption fell far behind that of national income. The difference between the growth rates of production and real wages was even greater, which led to tension in the factories with regard to salaries.

The smaller Comecon countries still depended on the Soviet Union's wealth of raw materials and energy, but problems arose in that country as well. The focus of crude-oil production, for example, was shifting from the shallow wells around the Caspian Sea to the inhospitable reaches of central and northern Siberia, where oil lay 2,000–3,000 meters below the earth's surface. The Comecon markets were now further from the oil fields, and the costs of production were rising. There were repeated observations that the material- and energy-intensity of production was irrationally high, that the products were unnecessarily heavy, and that energy was being wasted. For these reasons, and because of industry's sectoral and product patterns, the socialist country economies used more material and energy than did capitalist countries at similar levels of development.

To advance technologically, the nations of Eastern Europe had to expand their economic relations with the advanced industrial countries, but they ran up against several barriers. There was little demand for their goods and services; the capitalist countries took discriminatory measures against them, such as important limitations and high duties; and the marketing done by the large foreign-trade monopolies was extremely clumsy—it was not unusual for a mutually beneficial deal proposed by a Western business firm to founder simply because the appropriate person or office could not be found in time to sign the contract.

Nearly every country in the region pondered the need for economic change, and two types of reform emerged. The first aimed at "perfecting" the existing system. The plan directives would be simplified, the price system would be reformed, and profits would play a greater role in decision making. Enterprises would gain limited—very limited—control over investments, using state credits. Hungary's reforms in the decade after the 1956 collapse were of this type, as were the Kosygin reforms in the Soviet Union.

The second type of reform went deeper. It was based on the belief that socialism was by nature a commodity-producing system and that central planning hampered both the domestic division of labor and integration into the world economy. Unlike reformers of the first type, the proponents of radical reform did not seek merely the "better use of the commodity and money categories": they wanted those categories to function fully in a market. The state's role would be limited mainly to macroeconomic management—controlling the money and credit supplies, setting wage and employment policies, and developing the economic infrastructure through education policy, general investment projects (roads, power, and the like), and large-scale industrial projects.

The roots of such thinking in Hungry go back to the mid-1950s, to a paper and book by György Péter, a prominent economist and chairman of the Hungarian Statistical Office, and a book by János Kornai in which he offered an empirical look at the economic behavior produced by plan directives.[37] Similar papers began to appear in Czech and Polish journals, and by the early 1960s, the team of experts who drafted the Prague Spring economic program had been formed in the Czechoslovakian Academy of Sciences' Institute of Economics under the leadership of Ota Sik. A book by Wlodzimierz Brus published in Warsaw in 1961[38] appeared in Hungarian in 1964 and greatly influenced the Hungarian reform movement. Yugoslavia adopted far-reaching reforms in 1965, developing the "socialism of self-management."

In Poland in the early 1970s, the plan directives dictated another round of stepped-up growth, and the resulting failure paved the way for the economic collapse of 1980 and military dictatorship. Czechoslovakia launched an economic reform in 1967 that was in many ways simliar to the Hungarian program begun the following year, but in Czechoslovakia, the reform went beyond economic goals. Opposition surfaced to the communist party's dominance and to the country's membership in the Warsaw Pact and Comecon. The Soviet Union felt that its global political interests were threatened, and after negotiations among the allies, Soviet, Bulgarian, Polish, East German, and Hungarian troops entered Czechoslovakia in 1968 to "prevent the overthrow of the socialist system." After that action economic reform languished. Some of the measures taken in 1967 existed only on paper after 1969; the plan-directive system functioned once again.

Hungary, then, acted alone in 1968 when it abolished mandatory plan directives, and this isolation proved to be an enormous handicap. Had other Comecon countries taken similar steps in the late 1960s, the Hungarian reform might have been strengthened. The internal and external restraints might have been fewer and weaker, and perhaps the Hungarian economy would have been healthier in the second half of the 1980s.

The Reform

In the first half of the 1960s, the performance of the Hungarian economy was far from spectacular. Output grew a mere 4 percent on average from 1961 to 1965, personal consumption by 3.5 percent—both lagging behind the results of the previous five years (6 and 5.5 percent, respectively). There were other signs of deteriorating performance. There were problems in finding the investment and raw materials needed to reach the growth target. It was clear that labor would soon be in short supply; for the big industrial centers, a sharp labor shortage was projected. Planning agencies realized that the policy of growth by boosting investment and throwing ever-greater resources into production was a dead end; output and personal consumption could grow only if the value added per worker rose. To achieve this end, the product mix had to be improved and adapted to changing foreign and domestic demand, and firms had to be modernized. As it was often put at the time, the extensive sources of growth being exhausted, intensive sources had to be mobilized.

There was another diagnosis as well. There were scientific proofs that Hungary's methods of macroeconomic management, the organization of the country's economy, and the system of motivation based on personal relationships and interests were all hampering progress. The entire economic system would have to be revamped if the intensive sources of growth were to be tapped. Limited reforms were rejected, and the door to a comprehensive reform opened wide.

The blueprint for this reform emerged after a year and a half of work by some 200 experts—researchers, company officials, and members of the government and party apparatus among them. A May 1966 resolution by the Central Committee of the Hungarian Socialist Worker's party on economic reform was based on this work, and after a host of government decrees and resolutions to pave the way, the first package of reforms went into effect a year and a half later, on 1 January 1968.

The Reform Concept

To quote from the May 1966 party resolution:

> The fundamental idea of the reform of our economic mechanism is the organic link between central planning and management of the national economy and an active role for the market, for commodity relationships based on socialist (public) property of the means of production. This organic link is the guarantee that the main goals and proportions of the national plan will be decided centrally and their realization enhanced by a better combination of appropriate means. At the same time the market mechanism, i.e., the interplay of supply, demand, and prices as well as real

commodity relationships between sellers and buyers, will also play a larger role within the totality of mechanisms of the socialist economy. This means that a large share of decision making becomes the prerogative of individual firms and the domain of decentralized decision making is enlarged.[39]

This text highlights three features of the reform:

1. Day-to-day coordination of the economy would be left mainly to the market mechanism and the relationships among supply, demand, and prices. This was a conscious break with dogma going back to Marx that socialism replaces the market with central, all-embracing, social coordination.
2. Central economic management would have mainly macroeconomic tasks: fixing the main macroeconomic proportions, working out development goals, and seeing to their fulfillment. This was a departure from the state's constant interference in microeconomic events.
3. Firms, as buyers and sellers, would be active in the marketplace and substantially independent. This was a departure from the command economy's system of plan directives.

Such reforms are constrained by the existing state of the economy, imperfect knowledge, and the fact that change threatens the power and position of certain players. Every step involves a fight between different strata and is therefore a compromise. The effects of these "noise" factors can be felt in every aspect of reform; they usually reinforce one another, and the impact of any given one goes unrecognized.

In the rest of this chapter, I will present the reform as it unfolded and the measures that created a new environment for public (state and cooperative) enterprises. I will discuss company autonomy under the profit-regulation system begun in 1968; the wage system; credits and investments; and the legal standing and market relations of individual firms. There was a complete break from the system of plan directives, but there were also compromises, steps delayed or missed for one reason or another.[40]

Toward Firm-Level Autonomy and a Working Market

The most fundamental change for firms was the disappearance of the plan directives, which had established the compulsory output assignments and limits on resource use. There was an end to official coordination of relations among firms, which thus became market relations.

Under the old system of plan instructions, the manufacturing firm handed over its output for domestic consumption to a central distributor who—obeying a quota—distributed it among other manufacturers and retailers. Products for export had to be marketed through the foreign-trade company authorized to handle that particular product line. This method operation guaranteed a certain security of supply and made adherence to the plan directives (input quotas) easier.

The reform put an end to this system, and (with some exceptions) companies were allowed to seek out new domestic partners. There were some problems in the beginning, but they were not serious. A textile factory would sell the bulk of its production to a wholesaler in the textile industry—its old mandatory partner—even without being told to do so. The wholesaler, too, continued doing business as before with the state-owned retailers, although now as a "seller" rather than as a "distributor." The textile factory's inputs were provided by foreign- and domestic-trade companies that had been converted from the old import and procurement centers. The only difference was that "bringing claims in line with endowments" (balancing needs and possibilities) was no longer the task of some higher-level agency (the ministries of light industry or of foreign or domestic trade); the firms concerned resolved such matters among themselves.

Old relationships thus took on a market character. From the beginning of the reform era, there were direct contacts between manufacturing and consumer firms. Textile factories contacted department stores and makers of ready-made clothes directly, and similar direct contacts emerged in other spheres of the economy—for example, between engineering and steel companies. The establishment of these relations led to sudden changes in the adjustment of supply to effective (money) demand and in the organization of production, distribution, and marketing.

The foundation of wholesaling firms was shaken, and their turnover fell. They were too big and in many respects superfluous. Some fought back by offering better services, a wider variety of goods, and similar improvements, and these firms kept most of their customers. Others simply lost their customers. Still others tried to hold on to their monopolies by relying on old connections. They negotiated contracts that barred their old suppliers from dealing directly with consumer firms, and they placed large orders to soak up the suppliers' entire capacity even if demand was unsure. Many manufacturers, in turn, were happy with such contracts. They were simpler and more in line with the old way of dealing with only a few wholesalers and having large-volume shipments instead of many customers and many small shipments. Such practices often succeeded because imports were a minor factor and most of the wholesale firms could defend their monopolies. Consumers, for their part, often had to content themselves with late deliveries of goods that didn't match their orders. As a result, partial shortages developed even in areas where total demand was less than total (potential) supply.

Without antitrust laws there could be no intervention, and bringing the problem to some higher authority, such as a government minister, was like asking the fox to watch the geese. Such cases were used as a pretext to increase official interference. The more of them, the better the authorities' chances of "restoring order" and maintaining their power.

The reform did improve the conduct of foreign trade,[41] which was vital for a small, resource-poor country like Hungary, whose exports in the late 1960s amounted to 40–45 percent of national income. Before the reform, manufacturers almost always had to operate through the large state export-import companies, which were the only companies empowered to sign foreign-trade contracts. Since the relaxation of this rule affected trade with Comecon and Western countries differently, I shall discuss them separately.

While the Hungarian reform effort was coming to a head, dramatic changes were in the works in some other Comecon countries, and the Hungarian leaders believed, incorrectly, that their country would not be alone in pursuing reform. Instead, moves toward a market economy elsewhere in Comecon came twenty years after the Hungarian reform began—in Poland and perhaps in the USSR, Czechoslovakia, and Bulgaria.

Under the old system, trade among Comecon countries was determined according to a framework of plan coordination and government contracts. Countries issued plan directives to their firms stating the type and amount of products to be exported and what was to be received in return. Price negotiations were conducted at the government level, with Comecon prices based on world market prices converted from the dollar into the so-called clearing ruble at a fixed rate ($1 = 0.8 clearing rubles). World market prices are relatively easy to determine in the case of commodities traded on exchanges, such as steel and wheat, although differences in quality can complicate matters. But with machinery or consumer goods, establishing corresponding prices is almost impossible, so the representatives of two Comecon countries negotiating export and import prices generally had wide latitude in bargaining.

This bargaining cannot rely on actual market relations. The deal is struck by civil servants; it is a bureaucratic act and the result of mutual concessions; "I accept your high prices for Y if you accept my high price for X." Since negotiations are always bilateral, it is no wonder that the clearing-ruble prices of a given product vary greatly among Comecon countries.

Hungary had to accept this system as a given when it shaped its reform package. Basing trade on direct contacts between firms in two countries was out of the question, so large import-export organizations with exclusive market rights to a particular product (steel, machinery, textiles, food, and so on) had to be kept in business. The main impact of the reform on Hungary's Comecon trade was that representatives from the large manufacturers were brought into the government-level nego- tiations. They had a say, within the limits of the negotiation process, in fixing specifications, quantities, and prices, and it was therefore reasonable that the resulting contracts be binding on them.

But disputes arose in Hungary's hybrid trade delegations. Government officials, who knew that the other side was ready to make concessions in a different area or who were simply exhausted or considered the matter unimportant, might be willing to go along with a price that company representatives considered unacceptable. In other cases, the company representatives might try to increase export quantities but run into opposition from the government members because a suitable amount of imports could not be found to balance the accounts.

With conflict came efforts to push the company representatives into the background or even to leave them out of the process entirely. Government contracts were declared compulsory even if a firm's repre- sentatives had opposed them or had not taken part in the negotiations. Company representatives resorted to contacting foreign trading partners directly with information that could influence talks so that the Hungarian company benefited. As a result, the country's negotiating positions suffered.

Matters of prestige also entered into such conflicts. The government officials (most of them civil servants from the Ministry of Foreign Trade) argued that their positions and knowledge made them the only true representatives of state interests. Branch ministries—the agencies that supervised the individual companies—also got involved in order to prove their indispensableness.

In trade with the West, a few manufacturers were given the right to import and export independently, but they were the exceptions. Most of the turnover was handled by specialized foreign-trade companies. This issue had been hotly debated during the reform planning, with some people arguing that the major exporting firms had to have the right to trade on their own. Others argued that manufacturers lacked people who were knowledgeable in international trade, and it was this viewpoint that won out. These proponents warned that the movement of specialists from foreign-trade companies to manufacturers would weaken the trade com- panies and, most important, that the state's interests could not be guaranteed unless all foreign trade was handled from the center (foreign- trade companies are directly under the Ministry of Foreign Trade). The country's limited export capacity and high import demand, they said, called for such day-to-day oversight of the trade and current accounts to avoid large trade deficits and indebtedness.

Although the foreign-trade companies were retained, relations between the manufacturers and these companies were rearranged. In order to make manufacturers interested in profitable exports and economical imports, they were to establish direct contacts with foreign markets and foreign partners and have a direct role in negotiations.

Trade on commission played a major role in the new system. The manufacturer did not deal with a foreign-trade company as a buyer or a seller but authorized it to import or export certain goods for a specified commission. For imports, the manufacturer paid the forint value of the foreign-currency price of the goods plus the commission; for exports, it received the forint value of the foreign-currency price minus the commission. The commission agreement could include a clause guaranteeing that the foreign-trade company would take an interest not only in import and export quantities but in favorable prices and shipping conditions as well. It might also call for the manufacturer to be involved in dealings with a foreign-trade partner. The foreign-trade company might pursue export and import activities on its own account, with the aim of reexport, and could have domestic trade functions as well.

As with the reorganization of Hungary's Comecon trade, the reform of trade with the West gave firms more room to maneuver but at the same time created conflicts. The manufacturers' representatives tried to be closely involved with the deals and tried to assert their interests, not only against the negotiators on the other side of the table, but against their own foreign-trade companies. The involvement of specialists from a manufacturing firm was very useful, provided they spoke foreign languages. These specialists could emerge from their long years of isolation, add to their knowledge and experience, and establish and use contacts. These changes contributed to an upswing in innovation, and more patents were granted in Hungary than ever before. Hungarian managers began to think in European terms, comparing domestic costs with world prices, and they could get a look at new technolgies. But there were problems. As foreign-trade companies often noted—correctly, if with some exaggeration—some manufacturers' employees were traveling abroad despite their ignorance of trade and foreign languages, and they attracted ridicule from their trading partners.

A useful division of labor sometimes emerged. At other times, the manufacturer–foreign-trade company relationship was rife with conflict generated by divergent interests. The foreign-trade companies were not pleased that manufacturers were acquiring trade specialists who became well-versed in their field and able to spot weaknesses in the trade-companies' practices. Strategic interests sometimes conflicted, too.

Manufacturers began to realize that one-of-a-kind or small-batch quality products were more competitive than mass-produced goods and tried to adjust their output accordingly. This type of production was not in the interests of the foreign-trade companies. Their commissions depended mainly on volume, and small-scale exports were counterproductive for them even if those exports did have a larger profit margin. No wonder, then, that some foreign-trade companies tried to break their commission contracts. As an excuse, they pointed to the occasional failure by manufacturers' specialists in foreign-trade negotiations.

The beginnings of market relations and marketing activity, rather than mere product distribution, gave manufacturers a greater say, which was to the good. Unlike earlier, in the second half of the 1960s inventories overall grew much more slowly than output; i.e., the inventory intensity of growth diminished. Capacities were better utilized, the propensity to export grew, and export performance (mainly to the West) grew much faster than output. Hungary's terms of trade improved, and exporters and importers seized the opportunity this improvement presented. At the start of the reform, imports were greatly restricted, and licenses were given only for the quantities imported in previous years. But manufacturers showed increasing interest in imports from the West. In the case of capital goods and more sophisticated parts and equipment, the forint came close to convertibility; that is, products could be imported from the West for forints without serious restrictions. And although domestic manufacturers were still insulated by high tariffs, the first signs of import competition nonetheless appeared, weakening the position of a few large domestic firms.

But the most important development, unquantifiable though it is, was the change of attitude on the part of many manufacturers. Managers had new markets, indeed the whole world, opened to them, and emphasis on volume of output gave way to thinking about price, cost, and profit. Managers began to assess the position of their firms and to determine their tasks as defined by the market. In some firms, however, exposure to the international environment led to pessimism and calls for protection.

From Calculated Prices to Market Prices

In a market, prices arise from billions of transactions, and vice versa, those transactions are guided by prices. There is no true price without a market, and there is no working market without price. In a system of planning directives, this relationship does not exist. Products have "prices," of course, but they are determined and decreed by government. From a regulatory point of view, these prices serve the goals of establishing plan targets, measuring plan fulfillment, and controlling the activity of individual firms. They are insulated from the supply-demand-price mechanism. Consumer goods have prices as well because they are "distributed" among members of the society. Workers receive wages and with that money buy products and services. A system of directed planning therefore deals in calculated, distributive prices.

Before Hungary's reform, officially declared prices did not even reflect cost calculations. Indeed, some domestically produced raw materials and semifinished goods had prices that did not cover production costs; in such cases, the manufacturer received a government subsidy. The reason given for such low prices was "production policy"; for example, low prices for machinery would be an incentive for mechanization. In setting and achieving plan targets, price changes were a nuisance, and the central authorities were inclined to stick to the old prices even if rising costs justified a change.

The prices of consumer goods were typically inconsistent with the costs involved, and there was a chronic mismatch between consumer and producer prices. The difference was made up by a complicated system of turnover taxes paid by the retail trade sector and government subsidies paid to that same sector. Basic foodstuffs (bread, meat, milk) and fuel were heavily subsidized, and for some public services (rent on state-owned flats, public-transportation fares) the subsidy was extraordinarily high. At the same time, turnover taxes raised the consumer prices of clothing, tobacco, and alcoholic beverages to well above the producer prices. This consumer-price structure was justified by social considerations, which may have been well-founded in the 1950s but by the late 1960s were certainly not.

In addition, real import and export prices were out of touch with domestic settlements in prereform Hungary. The domestic prices of imported products were adjusted to the price of some domestic substitute, and export products were sold to a foreign-trade company at a price based on domestic accounting principles. The final settlement of the difference between actual import and export prices and their domestic equivalents was carried out by the foreign-trade company and the state budget officials. As a consequence, for domestic manufacturers and consumers, export and import prices had no link with the forint equivalent of the prices in foreign currency, and the relationship between domestic prices and true import and export prices had no impact on the economy.

However one understands the prereform "prices," the reform inherited the old structures of producer and trade capacities, public consumption, and foreign trade. This inheritance cannot be denied when considering what is to be done when a country tries to transform itself suddenly into a market economy—a country that has no real market prices and that suffers from distorted patterns of production, consumption, and foreign trade. The changeover may raise prices for many manufacturing firms, but state intervention would nullify the reform. But if the state does not step in, as firms lose money their capacity will decline, output will fall, and workers will lose their jobs.

The change in consumer prices has different effects on different levels of the population. A large increase in the price of basic foods (caused by the abolition of the state subsidy) and a decrease in clothing prices (the result of a cut in the turnover tax) mean a decline in the purchasing power of the poor and an increase in the purchasing power of the rich, because poor families buy more food and less clothing, relatively speaking, than do rich ones. There may also be a change in the structure of consumption. Demand might fall for some consumer goods, but for others it might rise abruptly, creating shortages. It is doubtful whether such shifts can be evened out through trade—that is, whether firms facing lower domestic demand can export their superfluous output in exchange for the necessary imports.

Real import and export prices can be converted—with a suitable exchange rate—into forint prices, and these prices used in domestic settlements. In this case, outside conditions influence the domestic market. A domestic manufacturer cannot ask more for its product than the import price of a similar item, nor would it sell its product for less than the export price. If the exchange rate is effective (i.e., keeps the trade account in balance), such conditions are useful as import and export competition inspire domestic manufacturers to greater effort in the domestic market, trigger a healthy selection mechanism, and help to establish mutually beneficial foreign trade. At the same time, there is the risk of shocks early on in the conversion. In industries that have strong import competition, firms may go bankrupt. When domestic prices are lower than the world prices, exports may siphon off so much that shortages and large price increases result. All of these processes could lower a country's productive capacity for years and produce large trade deficits and indebtedness.

On the one hand, then, the market mechanism rationalized production, consumption, and foreign trade for Hungary. On the other hand, the country risked market and price effects powerful enough to burden the reform process just as it was establishing itself: lower capacity utilization, unemployment (unheard of for years), falling output, declining consumption by certain groups in the population, a trade deficit, and rising national debt. Policymakers had to take this duality into account in introducing or reinforcing market mechanisms and decide whether, given the economy's present state, shock therapy or a more moderate, phased-out approach was indicated.

Although Hungary's economic problems grew in the years before the reform and the growth rate fell, the country was not in crisis. The leadership, fearing economic shocks, took a cautious approach, the more so because reform faced opposition both in Comecon and at home. It is understandable, therefore, that the conversion was low-key, including both a basic market character and "diluting" elements.

There were three main features of the price system introduced on 1 January 1968.[42] First, the all-embracing system of official prices was abolished. The new system included fixed prices, prices that were allowed to move freely between official limits, and completely free prices. Fixed prices were used in three areas: basic raw materials for industrial or agricultural use such as fuel, electricity, and fertilizers; basic agricultural products such as corn, milk, livestock, and meat; and basic consumer goods and services such as flour, sugar, bread, meat, drugs, beer, housing, and public transportation.

Prices moving within fixed limits applied to capital goods, manufactured consumer goods, and processed food (e.g., clothing and canned food). Methods of calculating these prices were specified, as were maximum profit margins. Within the limits, firms (including trading firms) were free to choose their pricing policy. They could apply the upper-profit constraint to an entire product group, so that a high price for one item could be balanced by a low price for another. Free prices applied to intermediate goods, fashion items and cosmetics, food produced by smallholders, and other public services.

During the first two years, as was expected, rigidities were progressively removed, and more products were permitted to be priced freely. Later on, however—reportedly as a reaction to the investment boom and subsequent price rises—price controls became more rigid again.

Second, in principle the new price system integrated all foreign-trade prices. Foreign currency spent or earned was valued at exchange rates of 60 forints per dollar and 40 forints per clearing ruble. This was a clean break with the previous practice, under which foreign-trade prices were held apart from domestic ones. The sudden change arose from the idea that the benefits of the international division of labor could not be realized without a working market. As a result, firms began to think about foreign prices and to weigh foreign-market possibilities.

Raw-material sources were classified as domestic production, imports from socialist countries, or imports from capitalist countries. The fixed price of these raw materials was the average price of the three sources, though in certain cases (such as textile raw materials) the domestic price was set at the price of the marginal (most expensive) source, namely Western imports. The rule was not applied consistently, however. Only two-thirds of the exports to the West had previously been profitable at the 60-forint-per-dollar exchange rate; the loss on the rest had been covered by government subsidies. It was announced at the outset of the reform that subsidies would be reduced yearly, but applicants succeeded in keeping them going. In addition, price decreases in foreign markets led to a "flexible" interpretation of the subsidy policy. Over the years, subsidies actually rose.

Hungarian manufacturers were protected on the import side, too. Partial import liberalization improved the chances that Western yarn, machinery, and other goods would be brought into the country, but tariffs of 20–40 percent eased import competition—if they did not eliminate it entirely. This protection, at first considered temporary, proved to be permanent, and its scope expanded steadily.

Third, there were two opposing views regarding consumer prices as the reform was being planned. One was that reform would have to begin with a general consumer-price reshuffling. Consumer prices, it was argued, should be based on real costs so that a direct link could emerge between producer and consumer prices. The system of differentiated price supplements and turnover taxes, which had caused consumer prices to diverge from producer prices, would have to be discarded, and reform offered the chance to do so. Compromise was possible on some products or services, such as rents and public transport fees, and it might take several years to phase out government subsidies. High turnover taxes and consumer prices might also be maintained for tobacco, alcoholic beverages, and luxury items. Price restructuring must proceed, adherents said, as the only way to rationalize consumption and the relationship between production and private consumption. The losers in this realignment (pensioners, factory workers) might be compensated.

Opponents pointed to the damage certain groups would suffer and the social tension that could result. They argued that the harm done to certain strata could be compensated only on average, and there would always be families who, because of their consuming habits, were hit harder than the average. Such families, many of them headed by factory workers, would find their standard of living dropping overnight, and the resulting uproar would discredit the reform.

Inevitably, the opponents argued, other people would benefit from the price realignment, so in the end there would be greater disparities in real income. On the one hand, there would be losses to be made up from the budget or from corporate income; on the other, total real income would grow. A consumer-price restructuring would thus inevitably transfer income from the state to the population. Therefore, it was argued, it would be unwise to revamp prices at the start of the reform; better to phase them in over four or five years. Losses and gains for individual families would not be so pronounced, and if real incomes grew in the meantime at an average rate of 4–5 percent, even major changes later in the consumer-price structure and in consumption itself might not cause serious tensions.

The latter view gained the upper hand, and the reform was launched without serious consumer-price reform. Major inconsistencies between the new producer and unchanged consumer prices were reconciled by adjustments to consumer-price subsidies and turnover taxes; in product categories in which producer prices grew considerably, for example, turnover taxes were cut or consumer price subsidies raised. Under the new system, milk and dairy products had price subsidies of 40 percent (in other words, producers received 1.4 times the consumer price), and the price of clothing included a 30 percent turnover tax (on top of the retailer's margin). Exceptionally low prices (compared to production costs) were maintained for coal, central heating, and public transport via subsidies of close to 100 percent. The authorities tried to reduce changes in relative prices within product groups, which reinforced the differentiating effects of turnover taxes and subsidies. Coal had 100 different turnover-tax and price-subsidy rates, clothing almost 200.[43]

The main novelty of the reform as it applied to consumer prices was that free prices, and to a lesser extent limited prices, could adapt to changes in supply and demand. But on the whole, relative consumer price changes were cushioned. Real costs did not have as much of an impact on consumer preferences, and thus on production, as they might have.

Moving ahead in time a bit, one could add that this problem continues to characterize the Hungarian economy. Leaving aside some corrections in the late 1970s and early 1980s (major price increases for fuel, electricity, rent on state-owned flats, and public transport), discrepancies between consumer prices and real costs persisted well into the 1980s. Hungary will eventually have to put things in order during a period when private consumption stagnates or decreases, that is, during a period when the conditions are far less favorable.

Decentralization of Investment Decisions

Under a system of plan directives, companies can make suggestions, but the central authorities make the investment decisions. According to this concept, the government has the necessary information: What products or services are in short supply, what needs will grow, what is planned elsewhere in the economy, and so forth. Foreign-trade forecasts should also be made centrally: What the demand will be for imports, and what export capacities should be installed to earn the currency that will be needed. (For investment in any Comecon-oriented capacity, these decisions are an outgrowth of government contracts.)

Decisions about major investments are made directly by the government, mainly the Planning Office; decisions about smaller investments, by branch ministries (within the limits set by the plan). Financing comes from the budget or central assignments, and central agencies dispose of even firm-level amortization. The firms' only task is to carry out decisions made higher up the chain.

Even so, companies are not entirely reduced to the position of onlookers. They try to manipulate events by passing along ideas or by trying to demonstrate how small their capacities are compared to real needs. Branch ministries, which want to promote their own interests, are the companies' partners in this effort. In their projections for capital projects, firms and branch ministries look for output to be as high and costs as low as possible. No wonder such projections almost never come true: Costs usually turn out to be higher than forecast, and output lower. Taking the people responsible to task is almost unheard of. So many agencies have a hand in a major investment project, so many small decisions are made during the planning phase, that the true culprits cannot be determined, and even if they could be found, responsibility is diffused so widely that it almost vanishes. In any case, three or four years usually pass between a decision on investment and its implementation. With many factors changing in the meantime, "objective" reasons can be found for almost any failure.

These problems have long been the subject of a vast literature, and giving individual firms the right to make major investment decisions was an important part of the reform. But what is "major"? What powers should remain in the hands of the central government, considering that today's investment decisions shape tomorrow's economy?

The reform planners debated these questions vigorously. Nobody denied that the share of investments within the GDP—that is, the total volume of investments—had to be determined within the framework of macroeconomic planning and implemented through macroeconomic regulation. Nobody challenged the view that the amount of investment in infrastructure (schools, hospitals, transportation, housing, etc.), as well as individual investment activity in these areas, had to be governed by the plan. But there was no agreement on the proper division of power between the center (the ministries of culture and health) and local government (councils on the county and municipal levels).

The most serious disagreements had to do with investments in the so-called competitive sphere—industry, agriculture, and trade. As indicated by the 1966 party resolution, the problem was how far major development goals, and thus the investment structure, should be spelled out in the plans and how much of a rule in shaping investment should fall to companies and the market.

There were two diametrically opposed views.[44] According to one, investments in the competitive sphere are an attribute par excellence of market-oriented corporate management. The firms themselves should decide on investment goals and the ways of raising the needed capital. The state's role, according to this view, is to influence the total volume of investment by monetary and fiscal means, which could include preferential (though publicly acknowledged) credits, lower rates of interest, or capital allotments for, say, 30 percent of the cost of an investment. The state has the power to set up companies, in which case its allotment would cover the entire investment. But on the whole, preferential credits and capital allotments would be the exceptions. In principle, investment in the competitive sphere should be part of each firm's independent strategy.

The other view favored large-scale government intervention. It stressed that while market signals are at most short-range, investment decisons must address long-term problems; these decisions determine the future structure of the economy. The government's job is to consider long-run effects and shape the economy consciously. This is the very area, it was argued, in which socialism holds the advantage. Medium-range (mainly five-year) and long-range planners must have the prime role in determining investments. The macroeconomic plan must set the main development goals for particular industries (for example, reconstruction of the textile or furniture industry) as well as other development goals (for example, new plastic-production capacities at a preset performance level) and the investment they require. The national plan coordinates investment demand from the competitive sphere with investment possibilities and determines how much of GDP may go for investment. Therefore, the plan has to outline how much individual industries (branches) in the competitive sphere should invest. It has to take into account how much money each industry has available and how much in loans and government capital allotments must be added to that amount. The figures can allow for small deviations in either direction, but investment policy should not be left to the firm.

Even according to this view, firms would have a say in their investment programs. A firm of average profitability might replace its aging equipment (and in the process even obtain more advanced equipment) out of its own pocket. The more profitable the firm, the greater the opportunity for investment. A large part of the profit incentive would be that at a relatively high rate of profit, the company would have the resources it needed for small increases in its capacity. But the firms would still have to compete (within the constraints of the macroeconomic plan) for investment credits and capital allotments from the state budget. A company could repay principal and interest on those credits or make payments against the capital allotments if its investments were profitable. Thus firms would have to consider profitability in deciding on investment projects. On this basis, some investment decisions could be decentralized. At the same time, the state would regulate the overall structure of investments and the development goals, even in the competitive sphere.

The differences between these two viewpoints went beyond investments, and these underlying differences came to the fore as the reform proceeded. The first concept works only if capital is allocated on a market basis. The market distinguishes between the profitability of individual firms: Some go bankrupt; others make profits that exceed their normal investment needs. A rational use of bankrupt companies' assets or the reallocation of resources according to profitability requires the unimpeded flow of capital. But capital cannot flow freely without forces working to increase wealth (capital). Firms must be motivated to preserve and increase their assets, and there must be institutions that specialize in collecting money and lending it out as capital. There is a need for a network of trading banks run on business principles under the guidance of a central bank responsible for the economy's money supply.

In the second view, every firm must earn a modest and more or less equal profit. A firm's investment resources must cover the replacement of equipment with updated technology, but not significant increases in capacity. Since firms will want to invest in themselves, most profit should be centralized by monetary and fiscal means. Business criteria must be used in distributing credits or capital allotments; the recipients must pay back their credits with interest, or the capital allotment with a dividend. The dual task of allocating capital according to central goals while lending according to business criteria can be accomplished only by a central bank that creates money, distributes credit and capital allotments, and sets the business criteria.

The first approach would have entailed far greater changes in the economic system than the second, so it is hardly suprising that the second prevailed. Thus the reform perpetuated the system of centralized capital allocation even in the competitive sphere. Such a reform was in line with existing interests. The central economic authorities, including the branch ministries, could approve or reject firms' initiatives, decide on investments, and "administer justice" in difficult cases (for example, should the Ministry of Steel and Engineering Industries lend its machine-tool firms 2 billion–2.5 billion forints in the current five-year period or 4 billion–4.5 billion?). This element of the reform maintained (perhaps one should say salvaged) the central bureaucracy's power over fundamental economic activities.[45]

The reform's provisions for investment meshed uneasily with the market forces, and even in the competitive sphere, plan bargaining survived:

Firms could challenge the credit lines and capital allotments determined by a plan, and such bargaining affected other areas of the economy. As I have mentioned, this version of the reform implied moderate profits, which were not greatly differentiated among firms. This result, coupled with large-scale capital reallocation by the state, meant that a large share of the profits and even of amortization had to be centralized. The distribution of capital according to both government goals and business criteria penalized growing firms that were not yet making even moderate profits. The system therefore implied state manipulation of individual companies' activities and profits through taxes, credits, and similar tools.

Labor and Wages

The system of plan directives involved control of labor. Plan instructions prescribed, among other things, the number of workers and the total wage bill. It was clear from the start of the reform that firms could not be told how many people to employ, but wages were a different matter. Hungary's labor shortage had to be taken into account, and in addition, since the first years of reform would see only the beginning of market competition, the firms' cost sensitivity would be low. A sudden liberalization could cause wages to skyrocket, risking inflation—and inflation is easier to start than to stop. Wage increases, then, had to be controlled, at least temporarily.

There were, again, two schools of thought. The argument turned on the question of whether, in a reformed economy, workers in state and cooperative firms could think like owners and subordinate their immediate interests to the good of the company. One argument held that while nonmanagement employees (blue- and white-collar alike) in a large firm can be made responsible for and (through their wages) interested in doing a good job, they will not put the firm's interests first. Also, workers who cannot do their jobs must be let go; this solution may be the best one for the firm and for society at large, but it hardly encourages workers to take the long view. A firm could have a profit-sharing system, but profits paid out in this way could not be a large share of the firm's income. Profit sharing, the argument went, is more a noble gesture than a source of income.[46]

The other view held that workers could acquire a proprietary outlook. They could get to know their workshop or plant well enough to come up with ideas for improvements—how to reorganize production, for example. Give workers a role in shaping their environment, and their creative energy will surface. In a society based on socialist property, it was argued, such worker participation is a natural phenomenon and could best be ensured by linking worker's income to the firm's profits.

In the end, a wage-regulation (or, more precisely, income-regulation) system was introduced that was more or less consistent with both of these lines of thought.[47] Under this system, employee income was divided into two parts: the wage fund and the so-called incentive fund, the latter financed from profits. Together, the two funds set the upper limit on firm-level personal income. Other than that, companies had a free hand concerning wages. They might pay wages from the incentive fund and bonuses from the wage fund and, after the balance was closed, distribute the profits on a shared basis.

A key element in this system was each firm's average yearly wage in 1967, as the intitial wage fund was established at the average 1967 wage multiplied by the average number of employees. Figured this way, the wage fund moved parallel to the yearly average staff level, so hiring was not regulated per se. But the system also tied the wage level to the composition of a firm's work force. If less-qualified workers were hired— those whose wages were below the average—then the increase in the wage fund could outperform the wage claims of the new employees and the difference could be paid out to longtime employees. By the same logic, hiring well-qualified (high-wage) workers or firing lesser-skilled (low-wage) ones could be detrimental to a firm.

The size of the incentive fund in relation to the wage fund was a function of profits. To simplify the matter somewhat, the higher the rate of profit, the greater the incentive fund. In this way, the system related workers' income to the profit level. But the relationship was not very strong since progressive taxation narrowed the variation in profit levels among firms. Consider this example: At a 20 percent profit rate, an incentive fund amounted to 7 percent of the wage fund, but at profit levels of 10 percent and 5 percent, the figures were 5.5 percent and 4 percent, respectively. (That is, 1:2:4 profit volume ratios are associated with 104:105.5:107 income ratios.) Each firm that did not fall behind its previous year's profit level won a yearly 2 percent increase in its wage and incentive funds. The state guaranteed all workers in money-losing firms their previous wages. High-level management personnel were guaranteed only 75 percent of their base wage rate; middle-level management, 85 percent. On the other hand, compared to ordinary workers, high-level managers were entitled to a four-or fivefold dividend when a firm made a profit; middle-level management, a two- or threefold dividend.

This system of income regulation was the second element in firm-level profit motivation (the first is discussed in the section on investment), and the experts who wanted to cultivate proprietary attitudes in workers favored this type of regulation. They stressed the importance of an incentive fund depending on profits, believing that its role would expand while wage controls would gradually disappear; differences in the profitability of firms would then translate into large differences in wages, which would help make companies all the more conscious of the market.

The experts who took the opposing view were pleased that incentive funds did not vary much among firms and did not want to see things change. They assumed that as market forces gathered strength, labor supply and demand would move toward equilibrium. In combination with stronger competition, this situation would allow wage regulation to be relaxed without sparking inflation; eventually, wages could be left to bargaining between employees and employers.

However cautiously income was regulated, it created problems during the first two years of reform. Inequities in the first year of profit sharing (1969) led to discontent, and a storm arose when firms in bad financial shape found themselves unable to raise wages more than 1–2 percent for two years in a row while others were raising wages by 6–7 percent annually.

Policymakers reacted in two ways. Some, with the support of such institutions as the Planning Office and the Ministry of Finance, held that these problems were the inevitable birth pains of reform. Others (including people in the branch ministries and the middle-level agencies of both the central government and the Hungarian Socialist Workers' party) pressed successfully for immediate action. Some firms won tax exemptions, government subsidies, and special permission to replenish their incentive funds. As it turned out, income regulation proved to be a key in the development of the entire regulatory system. The rules were often changed, exemptions were frequently made, and there were numerous cases of government intervention to benefit particular firms. Economic policy could not fully incorporate the idea that workers' income should depend on a firm's profits.

The Institutional Structure and the Legal Standing of Firms

In planning the reform, a problem arose of whether Hungary's economic institutions, created in the era of directed planning, were appropriate for commodity production based on both central economic management and an active market. The question had two dimensions: the institutions of central management and the corporate structure.

The system of central management included institutions designed along functional and sectoral lines. No one challenged the existence of the functional agencies; in fact, the reform spelled out the tasks of the Planning Office, the Ministry of Finance, and the Ministry of Foreign Trade. Nor did the reform plan, particularly in the preparatory stage, question the role of the Price Office or the Ministry of Labor. I have already noted that regulation of sectoral investments demanded a unified banking system—the Hungarian National Bank—which would also have monetary and credit functions.

Sectoral division was another problem. Under a system of plan directives, a proliferation of branch ministries and related offices was inevitable. They were needed to flesh out plan objectives, because only such agencies could determine input and output targets on the firm level. Prereform Hungary had seven sectoral ministries (steel and engineering industries, light industry, etc.); within these were specialized units (a department for the textile industry, for example, and within that, offices to oversee cotton, wool, and silk production). The reform did not need such agencies, and it was common knowledge that if allowed to survive, their employees would inevitably cling to power by creating work for themselves.

The reformers, knowing the political obstacles involved, did not stage a frontal assault on these ministries. They wanted to win them over, or at least not to make enemies of them. In their own fields, the ministries were given control of research, education, and development spending, and in their role as "owners," they had significant control over the state companies. A minister (or the ministry acting in the minister's name) could create or liquidate these firms by decree; determine the broad outlines of their structure; and hire, pay, and fire their chief executives. At the same time, the reform provided that one, the chief executive officer (CEO) and the firm would be responsible for the plans of the enterprise and their modification for preserving, using, and increasing the firm's assets and two, the ministry could issue orders only in unusual cases, such as when national interests were at stake and results could not be obtained by economic means.

A ministry's property rights were thus kept in check. With less to do, the branch ministries saw their authority and staffs dwindle. Many subbranch departments were closed down, and the branch ministries' work force was reduced by 30–40 percent. This arrangement was a major factor in keeping the ministries from overstepping their authority.

Hungary's corporate structure bore the stamp of the old planning system. I have noted that in the years preceding the reform, reorganization created an overly centralized corporate structure—many large firms with four or five plants apiece and almost no small or medium-sized companies. It was clear to the authors of the reform that monopoly and oligopoly would hinder a competitive market, but the problem was delicate. The government-sponsored merger campaign was only a few years old, and a sudden about-face would not be well received. Many economists suggested that the reform need not undo the mergers altogether.

As a result, except for dissolving some big trusts, the reform left the structure untouched. The idea was that with the help of the government in its role as owner, individual plants could win some independence within the large companies. Indeed, the first years of the reform saw a wave of decentralization and an increase in the number of state firms.

It was crucial that the reform opened up opportunities for firms and cooperatives to branch out into new areas. Cooperative farms took on sidelines, increasing their revenue and stabilizing employment for both their members and others in the countryside. As early as the mid-1960s there were cooperatives with facilities for food processing, machine repair, construction work, and marketing. During the first years of the reform, some of them expanded these businesses and launched new ones—this time, to meet outside demand. The movement gained momentum as entrepreneurial types with the means and know-how set up small plants under the aegis of a cooperative. These plants were obligated by contract to turn over part of their profit to the cooperative. Beyond that, they were free to act as they wished. Such ventures under the cooperative umbrella (most small, some medium-sized) were usually established near cities, where the demand for parts and equipment, consumer goods, and services was the greatest. Small businesses thus strengthened the corporate structure.

The cooperatives' sidelines generally used local labor—something there was plenty of if only because of the seasonality of farm work. Some of the entrepreneurs and skilled workers came from large firms, attracted by the much better pay (even if the work was harder) and the varied work that made better use of their skills. Although such mobility was not common (even firms hit the hardest lost only 2–3 percent of their workers), it cost large firms their most skilled and versatile employees. The companies considered this mobility a direct affront and complained that those "abominable little shops" were keeping them from operating to their full capacity.

Summary: Progressive and Regressive Trends

The reform begun in 1968 turned companies and former planning officials alike into market actors. It did away with bargaining for plan targets and resources and the concern for plan fulfillment, the driving forces of economic activity under the previous system. Firms and their managers began to think in terms of market shares, prices, costs, sales, and profit prospects.

The effects of the new, more rational system were soon felt. The energy and raw-material intensity of production fell, and as a result GDP grew faster than aggregate output. Supply was much better adapted to effective (money) demand, so exports, including exports to the West, became more important. The terms of trade improved by 1–2 percent yearly, and foreign trade was more balanced. Firms also obtained more imported goods from the West with less trouble. Such effects, reinforcing one another, spurred economic growth. In the first period of reform, 1967–1971, national income grew by 6–7 percent yearly compared to the previous 4–4.5 percent.

This economic takeoff affected living standards. Real per capita income grew for five years at a constant 5–5.6 percent per year, or by one-third for the whole period. Because supply was better matched to demand, most of the consumer-goods shortages disappeared. As Hungary's current account improved, domestic-trade companies received limited permission to import Western consumer goods, which helped to stimulate the consumer-goods market. Rising income and greater supplies enabled more households to buy durable goods. Between 1965 and 1971, the number of refrigerators per 100 households grew from 8 to 39, that of washing machines from 37 to 59, of television sets from 27 to 58, of cars from 3 to 9. Hungarians won the right to buy convertible currency for travel elsewhere every three years, and many traveled to the West. (Citizens of other socialist countries, except for Yugoslavia, did not have the same opportunity until the second half of the 1980s.) All this activity raised the subjective value of the forint. People tried to earn more forints by working harder to produce higher-quality goods.

The economy emerging in Hungary stood in contrast to the economies of the more conservative Comecon countries. Kádár's international standing precluded a direct attack on the reform, but it was suspect in official circles and criticism occasionally emerged, either between the lines or openly. The consumer marketplace in Hungary, and particularly in Budapest, was rich compared to the markets in Prague, East Berlin, Sofia, Warsaw, and Bucharest. There were grumblings that "the Hungarians live too well," but a growing number of Eastern European officials began joining the tourists heading to Budapest to do their shopping. The city became a favored site for Comecon conferences, which helped to raise local living standards and improve the supply of goods still more. National pride began to crystallize around the reforms. Hungarians considered themselves the pioneers in putting socialism on a more humane course, pointing the way for the other socialist countries, including the Soviet Union.

The reform did have negative effects. If companies and former bureaucrats became actors in the market, it was still a deformed market. With the corporate structure largely unchanged, the domestic market was characterized by strong, artificial (because they were unrelated to the size of the economy) monopolies and oligopolies. The new, small-scale decentralization, the creation of small and medium-sized ventures, could improve this state of affairs but not reverse it. In addition, as I have noted, firms still faced constraints in their three main markets.

In the domestic market, they contended with fixed or only partly free prices, though price controls were slowly being eased. The lack of consumer-price reform was another hindrance in the domestic market. Trade with other Comecon countries was still based on government agreements, and the currency used, the clearing ruble, existed only as an accounting device. The reform could not overhaul that trading system; the only change was the inclusion of company representatives in the trade negotiations, but this arrangement became a source of conflict. Trade with the West was hampered by the fact that most Hungarian firms could not export directly even though, as we have seen, the commission system loosened this constraint somewhat. On the other hand, the reform did improve Hungary's foreign-trade position with small steps toward liberalization, but high tariffs muted import competition.

These peculiarities meant that market functioning at the start of Hungary's reform was primitive and strongly distorted. It was not even distorted consistently, since different constraints applied to domestic, Comecon, and Western transactions and the interrelations among the three markets were weak.

Within the rules, different firms had vastly different opportunities to act independently. A company whose products were priced freely obviously had more room for maneuvering than one producing fixed-price goods. A firm producing for the Comecon markets under government contract operated differently than one producing mainly for the domestic market—not to mention one competing on Western markets, as those firms faced not only strong competition abroad but discrimination against products from socialist countries.

Central planners cannot cure the ills of a distorted market. If they try, the economy will wind up being driven by firms' efforts to obtain favorable treatment. If the planners do nothing, some firms will prosper while others suffer. A company with a stable market in the Soviet Union, secured by government contracts at favorable prices, may be in very good shape compared to one just starting to penetrate the West German market. Thus it was a firm's initial position that determined whether its managers preferred competition or government intervention. Managers' personalities also played a role. Flexible managers, able to exploit market niches, favored the freedom of the market while others better versed in bureaucratic strategy favored intervention.

The feature of firms learning to be motivated by profit was rational on the whole, particularly in contrast to the previous concern with plan fulfillment, but it was not without drawbacks. The profit motive had two sides: Profits were the source of the investment fund as well as of the incentive fund that went to pay workers. I have shown how the reform constrained the profit motive. On the investment side, the sectoral structure of investments was still determined by the government; the investment authorized on the firm level was little more than a technically sophisticated form of replacing old equipment. The autonomy of firms was sharply limited on the incentive side as well. As a result, the state had to use taxation to centralize the bulk of company profits. This method of operation causes serious problems if the financial burden of credits and government allotments for centrally planned investments falls on the firms themselves.

These distortions were the weakest elements of the reform because they precluded true capital and labor markets. The full extent of the problem was realized only in the late 1970s (although it was to some extent recognized in theoretical articles before then). The distortions became the most important problem of the reform in the 1980s: How, within the framework of commodity production, can the capital function—or, to put it differently, the asset motive—be reestablished.

A modern market economy cannot function without the integration of the commodity, capital, and labor markets. If the current state and future prospects of the commodity market have no impact on the capital market, then the mechanisms by which the commodity market produces equilibrium will fail. Movements in the capital market create new businesses and liquidate old ones, so they are important in the workings of the labor market. The composition and skills of the work force are in turn major determinants of capital movement. These relationships were not taken into account during the planning of the reform; it was thought that the burden would fall on the commodity markets alone.

Thus the first few years of the reform were filled with both economic success and tensions.[48] The preparation for the second stage of the reform was in progress, and proposals were being made for the elimination of artificial monopolistic positions and the decentralization of the organizational structure of enterprises, on how to reorganize the banking system, and on restructuring the system of economic state management. The whole problem of how to bring strong market forces in motion in the allocation of capital and labor was being investigated.[49]

The successes and tensions materialized, of course, in different ways for different people, which resulted in a certain amount of conflict. The interests of the old trading companies, which were trying to protect their monopolies, differed from those of manufacturers, who were trying to establish trade themselves. There were managers seeking more freedom and managers seeking more protection, and there was tension between company and government officials. But the main obstacles to reform lay in the government and party bureaucracies that had supervised the corporate sector during the era of directed planning. These people saw not only their power but their livelihood at risk, and they sought a solution in a stronger role for the state and curbs on the "excesses of reform." They did not propose an outright return to plan directives—that would have been politically unacceptable. Without attacking the basic ideas of the reform, they argued that firms still could not be left to their own devices, that they still needed central direction—not through plan instructions, but through regulations geared to national priorities. The direction of economic policy was in the balance, and a few years after the reform began, certain events made the debate more topical than ever.

5

Push for Growth and the Aborted Reform (1972–1978)

A Policy Challenge from Outside

The world economy did not change greatly during the first years of Hungary's economic reform. There were conference papers and other articles warning that energy and raw-material sources in the industrialized European part of the Soviet Union would soon be depleted and that exploitation would soon have to move to more remote, capital-intensive sites, which would be costlier in terms of both production and transportation. But this problem lay in the future. For the moment, trade among the Comecon countries continued to provide the smaller countries of Eastern Europe with most of the energy and raw materials they needed for growth. The Soviet Union delivered these materials at low prices (with regard to world market prices) in exchange for traditional, low-quality manufactured goods. The capitalist world market was in very good shape—almost trouble free, despite Club of Rome prophecies and minor shocks and uncertainties in foreign exchange—and Hungarian firms were able to increase their agricultural and manufactured exports to the West. Hungary's trade with capitalist countries was nearly balanced, and its volume grew rapidly.

The calm was short-lived. In December 1971, Comecon adopted the Comprehensive Program. Designed to strengthen the region's self-sufficiency, it declared that the Soviet Union and its satellites were to reinforce and "stabilize" their economic relations. It was an attempt to integrate the region at the level of medium-term national macroeconomic plans. Specialization and cooperation were to be based on contracts between governments, and increases in the production of individual products would be based on aggregate demand in Comecon, so that each country could concentrate its efforts on areas defined in the interstate agreements. Under this program, Hungary expanded its production of buses, for example, but refrained from making automobiles. Instead of the latter, it took part in Soviet car manufacturing as a subcontractor for certain parts (such as windshield wipers).

Comecon autarky had to reckon with the considerable increases in costs and capital intensity that were foreseen for energy and raw materials from the Soviet Union. With this problem in mind, the group embarked on collective investments and capital contributions to big (mainly Soviet) projects. Hungary and other Comecon countries participated in Soviet investments in pulp mills, asbestos production, and the Orenburg gas pipeline, for example. So-called long-term target programs were set up to promote specialization, cooperative endeavors, and shared investments. In the second half of the 1970s, target programs were established in energy and raw-material production, agriculture and food processing, and engineering.

The same era saw drastic changes in the capitalist world market. In August 1971 the United States announced it would no longer exchange dollars for gold, and in December the dollar was devalued. The international monetary system established in 1944 at Bretton Woods thus unraveled. Soon after, the oil price shock set the stage for far-reaching changes in international price relations. Oil prices rose 150 percent in 1973; by 1977 they stood at four times their 1970 level. The newly industrializing countries of the Third World established extensive textile, clothing, and steel-making capacities, forcing down the relative price of such goods worldwide. Early in the 1980s the "green revolution" and the European Economic Community's agricultural protectionism had the same effect on food prices.

The industrial countries' response to these changes was structural adjustment. These nations were creating the high technologies of the third industrial revolution, reducing the role of traditional manufacturing and turning to processes that conserved energy and raw materials. There were a few hard years, but on the whole these nations benefited from the change. Demand for their products and services grew, and "knowledge intensity" translated into high prices on the world market.

With hindsight, it can be seen that Hungary in the early 1970s had two choices.[50] The first was to adapt to the world economy and limit participation in Comecon's Comprehensive Program, regardless of the political and (in the short run) grave economic consequences. Hungary's economy was Comecon oriented, and a break could cost the country not only its secure supply of energy and raw materials but the tightening of export possibilities as well. The risks of this option, then, included inflation, changes in relative prices, further differentiation between firms, bankruptcies, unemployment, and a slowdown in growth or even a recession. There would be understandable resistance from those members of the ruling class who felt that their positions were in jeopardy. This course of action, though inherently more difficult in the short run, would have both needed and resulted in the fast development of the reform.

The other option was to stay firmly anchored to Comecon—contributing capital to secure energy and raw materials, maintaining Hungary's growth rate, and perpetuating a system in which government interference coexisted with the market. This course of action would involve central management of the economy, albeit without plan instructions, and (relying mainly on the initiative of individual firms) cautious cooperation with the West. Hungary would wait until the other Comecon countries moved toward establishing their own market economies and then reform its relations with them. This choice entailed the survival, though in different forms, of methods that had been proved to be inefficient and resulted in a reduction of the economy's development potential.

Standstill and a Quiet Step Backward

Several years after it began, the reform in Hungary had come to a turning point. Would events hasten the rise of a market economy, or would the government's role be pervasive? The question became more important as the problems with the early phase of the reform became evident and the challenges from the world market demanded a response.

There is no point trying to decide which affected Hungary's decision more, the situation at home or abroad. It is far more important to recognize that the answer to one problem determined the answer to the other. If conflicts and contradictions are solved case by case through government action, by "trimming the excesses" of the reform, then a stronger Comecon orientation and a slower opening to the world market were indicated, and vice versa: Adherence to the Comprehensive Program implied stronger government coordination of the economy. Similar considerations entered into the discussion of growth targets. Giving a high priority to the maintenance of rapid growth meant Comecon orientation, with its secure markets and prompt, individual solutions to conflicts. Movement toward a market economy meant more conflict and uncertainty, including uncertain relations with Comecon.

Hungary made its choice after 1971. It would cement its ties with Comecon, maintain its high growth rates, and reinforce the state's role in coordinating the economy. The reform principles developed in 1966–1968 were not thrown out in favor of directed planning, but firms would now have less scope for independent action, and the market's influence would be smaller than the reform had envisioned. The years after 1971 saw a quiet rollback of the reform along with a recentralization of decision making and the corporate structure.

This shift had a dramatic effect on the Hungarian economy. Measured in volume of output (at constant prices), the high growth rate continued, but foreign trade suffered because of deteriorating terms of trade so that growth was far slower in terms of value. Investments grew to an irrational size thanks to Comecon obligations, among other reasons. The ties to Comecon made Hungary's economy less flexible and hurt its competitiveness, which impeded adjustment to world market developments and worsened the unfavorable terms of trade. The country's debt grew day by day, and policy goals proved unreachable.

From a later vantage point, the turnabout of 1971 was wrong. It seemed at the time to be the simpler and less dangerous choice, the one that was better adapted to the existing economy. Some members of the leadership may have understood that "the thornier path leads further," but this was by no means the dominant opinion, and more radical steps toward reform were generally expected to meet with opposition from the other Comecon countries anyway.

In the remainder of this section, I will offer overviews of investment, labor, and wage policies after 1971 as well as of prices, the corporate structure, and the role of individual firms. The picture has been simplified and highlights selected features of the economy and their interactions.

Investment and Capital Allocation

During the first years of reform, there had been contradictions with regard to investment policy. Investment is a lengthy process, with decisions sometimes made years ahead of their implementation. When the reform began, investments that had been decided on long before were still in the pipeline—buildings were under construction, machinery was being produced or shipped. These projects reflected the beliefs, methods, and power structure of the era before the reform.

The reform changed the way companies invested. Using their somewhat increased autonomy and new financial muscle, firms placed investment orders that reflected their own priorities. As a result, the growth of investment in the early 1970s far exceeded what had been planned. Investments discharged in 1970 were 18 percent higher than the 1969 figure: in 1971, they were 10 percent higher still. One special problem was that sometimes firms refused to take machinery imported from Comecon countries under intergovernment agreements.

Government agencies reacted to such developments both economically and administratively. They reduced credit lines, raised profit taxes and other payments, and pressed firms to accept the Comecon machinery, supplying credits for the purpose. Branch ministries intervened strenuously, studying and reporting on corporate plans in what became an obligatory review.

Among other things, such reviews dealt with yearly plans. The members of the "ministerial jury" were high-ranking officials of branch ministries and other officials, including deputy ministers. Although the jury's decision was not binding, its very existence undermined the principle that corporate plans were the responsibility of a company's CEO. As noted above, the minister (or the ministry acting in the minister's name) was the CEO's employer, and if the CEO did not follow the jury's "recommendations"— there were a few such cases—he was bucking the chain of command.

The fourth five-year plan, for 1971–1975, was ratified after the reform was launched but before the Comprehensive Program was accepted, and its original investment targets imposed strict restraints on firms in the competitive sector. The investment structure was determined largely by big projects chosen at the government level, by so-called goal-oriented clustered investments, and by industry-level investment targets with associated credit lines. Still, the original targets left some room for profitable firms to spend their own investment funds, apply for credit, and make modest improvements on their own.

Soon, however, in line with the Comprehensive Program, almost all investment resources were channeled to large projects. Forty percent of the large investments originally slated were canceled and replaced with others three times as expensive. Individual investment projects chosen centrally accounted for 20 percent of the country's total investment allowance. These large investments were concentrated in the energy and raw-materials sectors, which reflected the pursuit of autarky, and other sectors were pushed into the background.

Beyond these individual investment projects, Central Development Programs were begun in petroleum-based synthetics, gas consumption, the aluminum industry, vehicle production, and the computer industry. One-fourth of Hungary's investment resources were spent on these programs in 1972–1978, not counting related auxiliary investments. Central Development Programs were all based on Comecon cooperation and served the Comecon goal of autarky. Comecon's orientation toward heavy industry did not change during the 1973-1974 oil price shock to reflect world conditions; in time, it was actually strengthened. Investments in import substitution were given preference in order to ease Hungary's dependence on Western markets, which reinforced the standing of the energy and raw-materials sectors and raised the economy's energy and raw-material intensities.

The fifth five-year plan, for 1976–1980, kept this same approach. A planned 30 percent growth in overall investment encompassed a 50 percent increase for metallugry, energy, and construction materials, a

20–25 percent increase for the service sector, and stagnating investment in agriculture.

The central economic-management agencies tried to control all investment, not just the large individual projects and the Central Development Programs. So-called branch-level development programs were put together; for example, there were programs to rebuild the textile, printing, and furniture industries. These programs were based on demand and technology both within Hungary and from other Comecon countries.[51]

Some Comecon-oriented investments were simply irrational. First, as products of bureaucracy, they were not market oriented; only by chance were they directed toward areas in which Hungary had a competitive advantage. Second, in an era of acute labor shortages, they typically involved large projects. Third, they were directed toward energy-intensive industries and used energy-intensive technologies at a time when energy prices were rising sharply and there were growing problems in the Soviet Union's energy sector. Further, they diverted money and labor away from investments in the mainstream of modern technology, projects that could have helped Hungary integrate more fully into the international division of labor and participate in the world market on a basis of comparative advantage.

But the damage done by investment policy cannot be reduced to structural problems. Firms lost autonomy in investment—it has been estimated that only 15–20 percent of manufacturing investments (replacements) were company initiated in 1972–1978—and after a few years of relaxation, the government was again in firm control of most investments and the system of capital allotments. The government-company hierarchy persisted, as did bargaining over investment limits.

Labor and Wages

Investment policy contributed greatly to high growth rates and the heating up of the economy. In the first ten years of the reform, investments grew (with fluctuations) by 8 percent, and investments as a share of GDP reached almost 40 percent, a very high level anywhere. This overheating strengthened the demand for labor because most of the investment projects were labor intensive. Many of the reconstruction programs noted above increased the demand for labor in industry, and there was almost no selection mechanism: Old, obsolete firms and plants did not close, and there were no labor-reducing investments. Under the circumstances, the labor shortage in the 1970s could only intensify.

Labor mobility—workers changing jobs on their own initiative—sped up. Both unskilled workers and those with convertible skills could easily find new jobs, and in most job categories workers could raise their wages by moving on. The ideal of full employment degenerated into overemployment and into wage competition among the enterprises.

The large industrial firms that had created many of the new jobs complained loudly, and the government took several actions in response. In 1972, workers at those large firms got an 8 percent wage increase. Limits were placed on the agricultural cooperatives' industrial sidelines, and some (including those near large industrial centers) were even ordered closed. Smaller industrial firms were merged with larger ones, and there was a wave of forced mergers among the industrial cooperatives in order to release workers for state-owned industry. Obstacles were put in the way of frequent job changers: They were allowed to take new jobs only for lower pay, they lost part of their paid vacation, their sick pay was reduced, and so forth. Temporary hiring freezes were imposed on companies deemed less important by local government. Officials also took charge of the movement of certain types of workers, funneling them to the large firms. The situation improved somewhat for the large companies, but only for a year or eighteen months. The policy measures were soon exhausted, with no lasting effect.[52]

When labor is scarce and companies not sufficiently cost sensitive, competition for workers drives up wages without increasing the supply of consumer goods. Prices inevitably rise, increasing companies' incomes and thus raising wages even more until inflation accelerates unchecked. Under the circumstances, ending or even easing wage regulation is out of the question.

As we have seen, the first principle of the wage regulation was that the more profitable firms should pay higher wages. There were obstacles to carrying out this principle, and because of the many exceptions made, the rule was effectively canceled. Two particular problems with wage regulation should be mentioned here. First, if firms' wages are centrally controlled, then firms cannot freely choose the combination of inputs that yields the maximum profit. Second, if wages are tied to profits or some other performance index, wage regulation creates disparities that lead to conflict and unjustified, even irrational, job hopping. During an acute labor shortage, disparities between wages at different firms cannot stay secret for long, and workers respond quickly and emphatically. The firm paying the lowest wages can lose a good part of its work force in a short time, and as a result, its capacity is underutilized. Beginning early in the reform, the rules were bent to make exceptions for particular firms, and eventually, the system had to be revamped.

Since there were almost annual modifications to the wage regulations, I will discuss only the conceptual changes. By 1971, the key to wage regulation was the change of emphasis to per capita value added—a sort of productivity index—rather than the profit race. Wages could be increased according to the annual rise in this index, and gradually, a firm's total wage bill for the year (the so-called wage account), rather than the average wage, was tied to it. Now and again, firms in a particular industry received permission to raise wages independent of the change in value added. From 1976 on, several systems were in effect at the same time: average wages dependent on productivity, total wages dependent on productivity, and average or total wage increases set by the central authorities. The central government determined which system applied to a particular industry, although firms could request reclassification.

Wage regulation, then, was rife with contradictions and unable to function without constant government interference. Firms whose wages lagged got special assistance or were reclassified to help them catch up; others whose wage increases were far above average were punished with reclassification or other measures. Disparities were flattened out in this way, but at the same time the government did not want to be in the position of deciding by how much wages could rise each year. It stuck to the idea that tying wages to performance was an incentive for rational behavior.

Other Conditions of Firm-Level Activity

The way Hungary regulated capital allocation, wages, and the labor market in the 1970s of course affected other aspects of the firms' behavior, working against market forces, reinforcing government interference, and recentralizing economic activity.

Centralization. Some of the forces behind the centralization of the corporate structure have already been noted in the discussion of the labor market. The macroeconomic policy oriented toward Comecon and rapid growth had a similar effect. Comecon trade was a large-scale affair, often involving many manufacturers at once, and large investments are best carried out by large companies. The tendency for companies to enlarge their monopoly position and to bargain with the government also reinforced centralization, as did the effort to "solve" problems by merging troubled state firms and cooperatives with more profitable ones. Centralization, then, took the form of mergers, the creation of trusts, and government intervention. The government could shape state firms in its role as owner, but it was able to impose its will on cooperatives as well.[53]

In the 1970s, a wave of centralization swept over the whole economy. Between 1970 and 1978, with increasing production and a constant labor force, the number of state firms decreased by 14 percent, that of industrial cooperatives by 16 percent. During the same period, the number of state and cooperative units in construction decreased by 34 percent; in retail trade, by 38 percent. A new agricultural production and organizational structure was also established, dubbed "the Hungarian model." A peculiar cooperation and division of labor between the large farms and small-scale agricultural production was characteristic of this model.

On the large farm end of the scale centralization was fairly strong, and between 1970 and 1978, the number of state farms was reduced by 27 percent; that of agricultural cooperatives by 44 percent. At the same time, the average acreage of state farms grew from 5,500 hectares to 7,500 hectares; the average for agricultural cooperatives grew from 2,000 hectares to 3,800 hectares. This organizational centralization had a strong technological background. State farms and agricultural cooperatives turned into large, mechanized production units, and industrial production systems—based on U.S. technology—were utilized in the cultivation of wheat, corn, etc. As a result, the per hectare yields of Hungary's large farms became only slightly worse than (and sometimes on a par with) those of the world's agricultural leaders.

There was also a large upsurge in the production and number of small and medium-sized agricultural units. The cooperation between the small producers and the large agricultural firms was strengthened, especially with regard to labor-intensive products (fruit and vegetables, animal breeding, etc.), and increased incentives and freedom for the small producers resulted in production that was better adapted to market needs.

Because of the higher yields on the large farms and the market-oriented activity of the small farms, provisions for the internal market were incomparably better than in any other Comecon country, and in addition, there were enough for a sizable export as well. In these years agricultural output grew by a yearly 4 percent on average. Within the framework of the large agricultural farms, market-oriented industrial and service ventures were formed. Thus the model of the mixed-profile agricultural large firms integrating a host of small farms—a successful model even in international terms—came into being.

Besides successes, this agricultural production and organizational structure had many drawbacks. Since cooperative members could not take in the whole of a cooperative's activities, their participation in management decisions became formal. In the late 1960s, the capital of the cooperatives had been declared indivisible, including the assets (land, e.g.) carried in by the peasants themselves, and trade in land had been abolished. Cooperative members became like wage laborers, and they were no longer interested in increasing collective wealth. The giant cooperatives proved to be inelastic and slow to adapt to the market, and their production costs were unjustifiably high (higher than in developed countires). Small-scale production on the other hand was (because of its size) unable to use modern technologies. This sector of agriculture still uses a great deal of labor; indeed, it wastes labor.[54]

Prices. Stronger regulations and "steering" by the state were employed to control all prices. One of the government's priorities was to keep producer and consumer prices from rising, so it attempted to suppress the forces that could push prices up. The world price shock certainly had its effect on Hungary's imports—the prices of Western and Eastern European raw materials and energy alike rose considerably—but the government allowed only a small part of these price increases to filter into the domestic market. Although import prices rose by an average of 50 percent (and export prices by 20 percent) from 1970 to 1975, domestic producer prices rose by only 15 percent and consumer prices by slightly more than 10 percent. Even in 1976, when outside pressures forced price increases, rises of only 7 percent in producer prices and 4.5 percent in consumer prices were planned. This action was taken at a time when the cost of imports was helping to push inflation in the industrialized market economies into the double digits.

Insulating the domestic market from the world price changes was convenient in the short run. Not much troubled by price increases, firms were free to pursue strategies that had been devised under the umbrella of government intervention. Government agencies were not forced to revise their investment plans, and Hungarians did not face a decline in their wealth or nominal income and did not have to adjust their consumption to changing prices. The leadership based its policy on the beliefs that the price changes were transitory and that Comecon could shield Hungary from the devastating effects of a capitalist world economy in crisis. Needless to say, the leadership made a costly mistake. Rising price subsidies put the government deeper in debt to the central bank, and even more important, the old structure of production and consumption was allowed to survive while the developed world and one part of its periphery, helped by market forces, were embarking on the greatest structural change of the twentieth century.

There were other inflationary pressures as well, for instance, the overheating sparked by Hungary's investment plans. Such a policy-generated boom has inflationary effects even in a market economy with abundant reserves. The pressures are all the stronger in an economy in which reserves are small, the ability to adapt is weak because the market is primitive, and most of the market actors hold monopolies. Nevertheless, stable prices were a promise and a priority. If domestic inflationary pressures were building, the government's answer was to reinforce the system of price control. Firms had to prepare annual pricing plans, even for products on which price regulations were not binding. Government officials discussed these plans with the companies and issued "recommendations"; any plans to change prices had to be reported. Price increases were often denounced as efforts to reap "undeserved profits" and reined in accordingly, even if high demand or the quality of the product justified the increase.

Commodity Market. A few years after the reform began, the commodity market stopped expanding and even began to contract, partly because of these changes. As government interference made pricing more rigid, supply and demand signals were disrupted, and foreign trade became more and more complicated. Contracts within Comecon, of course, were negotiated by the governments involved, but trade deals with the West also required government consultation since subsidies had to be raised constantly to neutralize the price increases on Western imports. As import restrictions grew, import competition died. The market's influence on investment declined as company independence was reduced. Recentralization of the corporate structure strengthened monopolies and reinforced the tendency of officials to inferfere with the market processes.

It must be emphasized that the market did not cease functioning entirely, nor was the system of central allocation restored. Companies still dealt with each other as buyers and sellers. When a manufacturer or an importer could not satisfy demand because of shortages or for some other reason, it would assign priorities to its customers or recommend substitutes. This situation meant in most cases that the manufacturer or trading company, taking advantage of a seller's market, assumed the role of allocating authority with the direct or indirect participation of the responsible government agencies.

The catchphrase in this seemingly market-based but rather bureaucratic system was "responsibility for provision." Responsibility for provision was the reason steelmakers produced a large volume of iron sticks for ferro concrete for the domestic construction industry when the world price was rising and exports would have been much more profitable. The government had to determine who got what when domestic demand, Comecon obligations, and Western export possibilities exceeded capacities by 15–20 percent. And it was responsibility for provision that forced the Hungarian cotton mills to produce diapers at a time when fixed consumer prices and increased raw-material costs meant they would lose money (social policy considerations kept the consumer price from being raised).

Allocation preferences and responsibility for provision are complex topics and include the many constraints on production and procurement, efforts to increase supplies, international obligations, efficiency and pricing problems, taxation, subsidies, and the different types of financing. The more important decisions brought together not only the agencies representing the manufacturers, the trading companies, and the consumers (e.g., the Ministry of Steel and Engineering Resources, the Ministry of Domestic Trade, and the Ministry of Foreign Trade) but also the Price Office, the National Bank, and the Planning Office. Local government initiated discussions when local problems demanded them or joined in at the request of local firms.

Such discussions turned into multilateral negotiations, a process of reconciling diverse interests. Firms whose products were acknowledged to be underpriced could receive compensation in the form of a preferential credit or approval of a long-pending import license. But financial concessions to solve pricing problems often implied concessions in return, in the form of delivery of products in short supply. In other cases, the Price Office made concessions in order to ease a firm's problems.[55]

The Indirect System of Economic Management

Among the issues the reform planners faced was finding a name to distinguish the new system from the old one of plan directives. Some experts suggested using the terms *indirect* and *direct regulation* to indicate that both were planned economies in which the state regulated important economic processes. The difference between the two was that under the old system, regulation was accomplished by direct order while with reform, only the general rules would be set centrally. An environment would be established to ensure that firms, in pursuing their own interests, advanced the interests of the state and society. Other experts favored the terms *centralization* and *decentralization* to indicate that while the old system had left most decisions in the hands of the central authorities, the new system would empower companies and other independent organizations to make them.

In the end, the debate turned out to be, not semantic, but substantive. The economic system established in the 1970s could best be termed indirect, but it was by no means decentralized. Although most economic decisions were formally made by the firms themselves, the government manipulated their environment and supervised their activities. For practical purposes, the firms were still managed by the government. I have already described the government's method of indirect management, but it is worthwhile to review the most important features, this time from the firms' point of view.

Inputs for individual firms were largely determined by a system of import licensing and the rankings set by the trading companies. As far as output was concerned, exports to fill Comecon contracts and the fulfillment of convertible export targets were practically compulsory. A large part of management's bonuses and ordinary workers' wages depended on fulfilling official "export expectations." Responsibility for provision meant that firms had to keep an eye on official plans for the domestic market, too.

Price regulations were crucial to the firms' financial health. There were import and export subsidies and indirect taxes, numerous officially fixed prices, and centralized accounting principles; in addition, the authorities kept a close watch on prices in general. Prices had to be discussed with the authorities and changes reported; the state might skim off part of a firm's profit by suggesting that price increases were "undeserved."

Wage increases at individual firms depended on the rate of profit growth. But the way the rules were applied made a difference, and that depended on how the company was classified and whether or not it won concessions from the government. It was hard even for financially sound companies to find investment capital on their own; they looked to be assigned some capital or to link up with a Central Development Program or some other priority project. A firm's financial condition was taken into consideration in fixing interest and other conditions on investment credits or capital allotments. A firm might also have the terms relaxed later on if it could show that its business environment had worsened or that its capital costs risen since the investment decision was made.

Indirect economic management subjected firms to two influences. On the one hand, they had to adapt to a distorted but still functioning market. On the other, prices, wages, taxes, credit lines, and other conditions of business might be influenced through bargaining. Being responsive to the market was good for business, affecting production decisions and their realization somewhat at the firm level, and some companies enjoyed spectacular growth under the new regime. The second influence—bureaucracy—helped perpetuate the old-style economy, though in a more or less modernized form. Government officials continued to reign over the economy, using market-economy tools to manipulate the environment in the absence of directed planning. It was still important for companies to know how they stood with the government and to wage the bargaining war skillfully. The difference was that under the old system, the struggle had concerned a firm's compulsory plan. Now it concerned prices, subsidies, the general rules for and exemptions from taxation and wage regulation, capital allotments, and maturities and rates of interest.

In Chapter 4, I presented three of the main ideas behind the reform. How did they fare under the indirect system of economic management?

1. "Day-to-day coordination of the economy would be left mainly to the market mechanism and the relationships among supply, demand, and prices." As it turned out, capital movements and investments were largely decided outside the context of the market. Economic actors could not completely ignore prices or supply and demand, but a firm's success

depended only in part on adapting to the market. Bargaining could also win profits and growth.

2. "Central economic management would have mainly macroeconomic tasks." This goal went unrealized. The government controlled the details of company activity through its "recommendations" and "expectations," the system of responsibility for provision, the setting of detailed investment goals, interference in the price mechanism, and manipulation of the regulations according to the financial health and growth potential of particular firms. The state's influence in the microeconomic sphere was reduced and its form altered, but it was not abandoned.

3. "Firms, as buyers and sellers, would be active in the marketplace and substantially independent." This goal was realized only formally, as we have seen, because of constant manipulation of the market environment.

Indirect management did improve the economy's performance to an extent. Government regulations no longer controlled all economic activity, market forces were given some play, and firms showed signs of independent judgment and entrepreneurship. Manipulation of business was much more restricted than in the era of directed planning and now used market tools. Price and credit concessions, subsidies, and exemptions from taxation or wage controls could be applied only within certain limits. Although the possibilities for government intervention were fewer, the system of indirect management allowed irrationalities that the reform should have discarded.

Red ink might put a firm in a difficult position, but it did not necessarily threaten its existence. The problem might be overcome by a change of business plans or by skillful bargaining with the authorities. Following a course dictated by the market was risky because the regulators might alter the rules of the game overnight. The relationship of government to business was still paternalistic. A firm succeeded if it responded to market conditions or if it attracted government support. In the latter case, efficiency requirements and financing problems suddenly lost their sting. With success hinging on the government's benevolence, firms developed insatiable appetites; macroeconomic constraints on growth, natural in a market setting, were no longer effective. The government had to use administrative measures to restrain wage and investment claims that would otherwise exceed the economy's capacity. Shortages persisted. A vicious circle was created that reinforced the firms' dependence.

Confusion arose from the fact that taxation, wage regulations, credit, and the like were controlled by different agencies, each issuing rules and granting exceptions from them. Coordination became ever more difficult, and it became clear that the system of indirect control was not serving its stated purposes.[56] The failure of Hungary's economic policy put a new item on the agenda: reforming the reform.

Doubtful Economic Performance

In the early 1970s, the Hungarian leadership opted for rapid growth and strong ties to Comecon. These were the top priorities in the fourth (1971–1975) and fifth (1976–1980) five-year plans. The macroeconomic data for 1971–1978 suggest that the choice was a good one. National income and GDP both grew at a fairly constant annual rate of 6 percent, and domestic consumption grew at more or less the same rate. Real consumption on the part of the population grew by 4 percent annually— during the ten years of the reform era, it grew by half. Hungary still had full, even more than full, employment. Gross investment grew by 8 percent yearly—double the rate of population consumption—and its ratio to GDP rose from 30 percent to 40 percent. The period was one of investment-led growth, and the statistics are especially striking for the period after 1973, when the industrial countries' growth rates fell and their unemployment rates rose substantially.

But this picture is misleading. The data on growth are for volumes at constant prices. They do not reflect price changes in foreign trade, which may affect particular countries favorably or unfavorably; for Hungary, poor in energy and raw materials, the price shock of this era was particularly harmful. Adding to the problem was the fact that Hungarian exports consisted mainly of unsophisticated goods from the metal, chemical, and textile industries—products that were becoming less valuable on the world market because low-wage developing countries were creating their own industries and flooding the market with similar exports. Hungary, with its existing economic and management system, was unable to adapt. There was also damage, with some time lag, when world price developments affected trade within Comecon. Hungary's Comecon trade losses were particularly grave because Comecon provided most of the country's energy and raw-material imports.

The trade problems show the other side of the story. Losses in foreign trade were so large that domestic consumption could continue growing only with serious current-account deficits. Consider the following data: From 1972 to 1978, Hungary's terms of trade deteriorated by 20 percent (that is, import prices grew that much more than export prices). In 1974 and 1975 alone, the terms of trade deteriorated by 16 percent. Imports and exports in those years made up roughly half the volume of GDP, so that the worsening terms of trade in 1978 meant a loss of 10 percent of GDP. As we have seen, domestic consumption in those years was about what the GDP would have been without the change in the terms of trade. The difference—the effect of changing terms of trade—was financed by foreign credits. The credit market at this time, an era of petrodollar recycling, was a buyers' market.

Hungary's debt grew to dangerous levels. Net indebtedness in hard currencies in 1976-1977 was roughly equal to one year's hard-currency exports. In 1978, exports for hard currency were only 80 percent of imports for hard currency, a deficit of more than $1 billion. Net indebtedness at the end of 1978 came to $4.8 billion, equal to a year and a half of exports.[57]

The government could no longer close its eyes to the problem and could no longer dismiss it as the temporary result of international developments. Hungary was on the verge of losing its creditworthiness. Behind the world market shocks lay long-standing structural adjustments that affected not only the Western markets but Comecon ones as well. Newly industrializing developing countries were gaining on their Eastern European competitors, and Hungary had to face up to serious structural problems.

As production grows, industry in a small country with few raw materials becomes more import intensive, and Hungary's import intensity was reinforced by the fact that to fill Comecon needs, its new industrial capacity was energy and raw-material intensive. (Technologies aimed at conservation were used only rarely.) Growing and differentiating private consumption added to the dilemma. Since the manufactured goods coming out of the old plants were fetching lower prices on the world market, Hungary had to export more and more in order to pay its import bill. Meanwhile, since the Comecon countries, including the Soviet Union, were showing little inclination to increase their exports, Hungary had to turn increasingly to the West and had to pay for a larger share of its imports with hard currency—at a time when the country's ability to export to the West was declining. Exports to the other Comecon countries had to be limited, which meant that capacity was underutilized. Hungary's deteriorating current-account position, debt, and ever-more-manifest structural problems led the leadership to reappraise priorities.

6

The Decade of Stagnation
(1978–1986)

Policy Intentions

The state of the economy at the end of 1978 and into 1979 led observers to prescribe a policy turnaround. They proposed a two-phase strategy: a consolidation period followed by renewed growth.[58] The consolidation was outlined as follows:

1. The first priority was to halt the deterioration of the hard-currency current account and the accumulation of hard-currency debt. These factors would be crucial in maintaining liquidity.

2. Hungary's creditworthiness could be improved by entering into international monetary and trade agreements and organizations. Hungary would have to increase its activity in the General Agreement on Tariffs and Trade (GATT) and take the necessary steps to apply for membership in the International Monetary Fund (IMF). (Hungary received IMF membership in 1982, which boosted its credit rating significantly.)

3. Domestic consumption had to be reduced at once in order to improve the current account. But in the interests of political stability, real wages had to be maintained or cut only marginally, for a 0.5–1 percent annual increase in private consumption. (Nonwage income was rising, if only because of the growing number of pensioners.) To restrain domestic consumption, investments—particularly investments in fixed assets—would have to be reduced considerably, a move also suggested by the high share of investments in the GDP.

4. Also to contain domestic consumption, domestic purchasing power had to shrink; in other words, a monetary contraction was needed. Long-term investment credit lines and government capital allotments would have to be curtailed and firm-level investment resources reduced. Other austerity measures would include accelerated credit repayment, the freezing of company funds, and the like. On the other hand, the system of nominal wage containment and wage regulation at the level of the firm

would not be radically altered. Therefore, the purchasing power of wages had to be kept down by slowly reducing the value of money—that is, by raising the prices of consumer goods. The government would elicit inflation and restrain it simultaneously. At long last the government could raise the price of meat, increase rents and public-transport fares, and the like and thus reduce the burden of consumer-price subsidies.

5. Companies seeking to utilize their full capacities could not be allowed to export goods to socialist countries beyond the limits laid down in the government contracts. Extra shipments could not be reciprocated, certainly not on terms favorable to Hungary, as the other Comecon countries had little to export; in any case, any surplus in the Comecon trade account would not be convertible.

6. A strong, lengthy monetary squeeze—the first in the history of planned economies—would encourage large companies interested in fully utilizing and enlarging their capacities to seek hard currency for their exports. Their efforts to increase hard-currency exports would lower export efficiency somewhat, but this result would be less damaging to profits than would a forced reduction in hard-currency imports. The latter option would create bottlenecks by making it impossible to use productive capacity fully.

7. Measures put off because of the derailment of the reform could now be implemented. These included changes in the producer price system that would help firms adapt to world markets and earn hard currency. (As we shall see, this was the purpose of the pricing system introduced on 1 January 1980.)

It was originally thought that consolidation would take three years. That was considered enough time to achieve cuts in domestic consumption and investments, better hard-currency export performance, stabilization of the current account, and thus stabilization of the economy, which could then resume its growth.

It is important to consider the extent to which the heralded "new growth path" would actually be new and how it was to be implemented. First, renewed growth was to be characterized by adaptation to the world market and stronger links with the world economy. Cooperation with Comecon would still be important, but Comecon technology was second-rate. Changes in the outside world would eventually find their way to Comecon countries, however, which meant that an early adaptation to the capitalist world market would improve Hungary's position among the socialist economies as well. Hungary would have to turn more to the capitalist world to satisfy its import requirements, the more so because the Soviet Union's ability to export energy and raw materials was declining.

Second, growth based on adaptation required major structural change. The amount of highly qualified labor and its ability to innovate would have to grow at the expense of mass production, and high technology would have to be applied to well-defined target areas. Therefore, large firms would have to be somewhat decentralized. There was also an urgent need for a network of small and medium-sized companies to serve as industrial and service support. The growth of the cooperatives and, within limits, the private sector could help in this regard.

Third, there would have to be a stronger legal and regulatory framework for international cooperation. The goal would be an attractive climate for foreign direct investment without sacrificing Hungary's management system or other interests.

Fourth, structural change should not affect the share of various industries in the economy; rather, it should improve the firms' product mixes. This improvement need not be brought about by large, centrally planned investment projects, but the central authorities could help companies that were trying to boost their exports by promoting such goals as rational energy use and by encouraging company proposals that favored innovative projects which would relieve bottlenecks.

Fifth, the 1980s could be thought of as a prolonged period of adjustment to the world economy. When the consolidation period ended there would be no more need for bitter economic medicine. At the same time, the natural growth rate of the Hungarian economy would have to be lowered to 2.5–3.5 percent annually instead of the previous 5–6 percent. Available resources (labor, raw-material and energy imports, high-technology investments) and demand (profitable exports for hard currency, exports to Comecon countries for "hard" goods, domestic demand constrained by current-account requirements) would not support stronger growth than that in an era of structural change. Such change would be investment intensive; so would the urgent modernization and expansion of the transportation, telecommunications, health, and education infrastructures. Investment would have to grow more in this phase than in the consolidation stage, which in turn would mean that private consumption would not increase by more than a modest 1.5–2 percent a year. Finally, all of these measures could necessitate a return to the reform process and, most important of all, to the guarantee of real company autonomy.

These proposals made up a realistic, coherent system, and the sixth (1981–1985) and seventh (1986–1990) five-year plans drew on them. It is safe to predict that the job will not be finished in the 1980s. The Hungarian economy was worse off and more vulnerable in the second half of the 1980s than it was at the end of the first half. Instead of improving, the country's current-account position worsened, and only dim signs of structural change and adjustment to the world market could be seen. The public could look forward, not to a mere slowdown, but to an outright decline in the growth rate of consumption.

Among the causes for the failure of the policy turnaround is, first, the fact that the leadership was not concerned enough about the possibility of trouble ahead and no reserves were accumulated. Therefore, restrictive measures were not strong enough and had to be reinforced from time to time. Second, the continuing subsidies to inefficient economic units diverted much-needed resources from viable organizations, and third, management changes in the direction of a market economy were made, but they were not strong enough to affect individual companies greatly or to strengthen market forces. The authorities, citing the country's current-account position, interfered constantly, thus strengthening the dependence of businesses on government and stifling initiative.

In the last section of this chapter I will discuss the causes of these developments, but first let us look at the state of the Hungarian economy in the first half of the 1980s as well as the major changes made in the system of economic management.

The Main Economic Processes as Reflected in the Data

On 23 July 1979, newspapers, radio, and television announced major consumer-price increases. Pork loin, for example, went to 73 forints a kilo from 58, beef round to 56 forints from 42, bread to 6.6 forints from 4.6, and cooking oil to 28.50 forints a liter from 22.

The increases did not take the country by surprise, since the party leadership had laid the groundwork skillfully. In the preceding months people had been introduced to the concept of terms of trade; they could understand official statements that Hungary was consuming more than it produced and that the oil-price shock had caused those terms to worsen. Better-informed circles knew in advance that the price of meat would go up 30 percent, flour 40 percent, rice 50 percent, and sugar 20 percent, and there were rumors that gas and electricity rates, rents, and trolley and bus fares would follow. People accepted, however grudgingly, the fact that a relatively prosperous decade would be followed by a few leaner years. Housewives went on a shopping frenzy in the days before the price increases, but the stores withstood the rush without running out of goods. After the increases went into effect, the political climate remained calm.

These and subsequent price increases were the first important steps in an economic policy aimed at equilibrium. They resulted in food prices that were on average 25 percent higher in 1980 than in 1978. In terms of total personal consumption, this increase meant a 20 percent rise in consumer prices. Wages (and peasants' income from cooperatives) rose in those two years by a nominal 15 percent; in other words, real wages fell during the period by almost 4 percent.

One-third of all personal income was in the form of transfer payments, and the government also provided free schooling and health services. The real value of these forms of income rose year by year—the most important transfer payments, the old-age pensions, were rising particularly strongly, partly because Hungary's demographic structure meant that more and more people were retiring. New pensions were considerably higher than the old ones, and the old pensions were raised to compensate for inflation. Total pension outlays in 1980 were 40 percent higher than in 1978, for a 20 percent rise in real terms.

All in all, transfer payments plus health and education services rose in real terms by 7 percent yearly, which meant that real income did not change much despite the fact that real wages were shrinking. Of course, this was still a major change from the days when real income rose 3.5–4.5 percent yearly.

Investment suffered the most serious cutback. Although the total volume of fixed-asset investments declined during this period by only 5 percent, gross investment (including inventory changes) plummeted by 20 percent.

The GDP grew 1.6 percent from 1978 to 1980 while domestic consumption fell 5 percent. In 1980, 98 percent of domestic consumption was covered by GDP realized (in 1978 the figure was 90 percent). The import volume fell by 5.5 percent because of tighter import licensing, and exports grew by more than 10 percent. Hungary took on debt much more slowly.

In 1981 and especially 1982, new foreign loans were hard to come by, and the interest rate rose to 14–16 percent. Interest on the outstanding debt doubled, and interest payments soaked up 20 percent of the annual hard-currency exports. The terms of trade worsened considerably in 1982. In addition, there were large withdrawals, mainly by the Arab oil countries, from the Hungarian National Bank, and bank reserves fell to the point where daily operations were endangered. Insolvency loomed.

The government increased its efforts to restore stability. Import restrictions were reinforced, and firms were ordered to increase their hard-currency exports by various one-time methods. In 1982 liquidity problems eased, production and consumption were on a par, and the hard-currency debt began to shrink.[59]

There were further improvements in 1983 and 1984 even though the terms of trade deteriorated by 2.5–3 percent annually, mainly as a result of the second oil-price shock. The GDP figure rose somewhat, and domestic consumption fell thanks to reduced investment, including investment in fixed assets, even though personal consumption rose. Export volume during the two years rose by 16 percent, imports by only 4 percent. The current account was positive despite the terms of trade problems. The net hard-currency debt fell by $1.3 billion from its 1980-1981 peak, to less than a year's worth of hard-currency exports. Special arrangements with the Soviet Union were partly responsible for this improvement. The second oil-price shock was hardly felt within Comecon, so Hungary could profitably sell to the West products refined from Soviet oil. Hungary also earned $500 million yearly in this period from its dollar-denominated trade with the Soviet Union, in which the Soviets bought agricultural products, mainly wheat and meat.

In 1984 the leadership decided that the lean years could end and eased a number of regulations, including wage controls and import licensing. The rate of inflation fell, and firms were given more autonomy in their investment activity. Real wages in 1985 and 1986 proceeded to grow by 3 percent, personal real income by 5 percent, and gross investment by 2 percent. Domestic consumption in 1986 was 4 percent above the 1984 level. On the darker side, the GDP produced rose only 1 percent during the two years. Export volume fell (hard-currency exports dropped by 10 percent), imports grew, and the terms of trade deteriorated by 4.5 percent (by 8.5 percent in hard-currency trade). The trade problems were caused by a rapid decline in world agricultural prices—wheat and meat prices fell by 40–50 percent because of large U.S. and European Community surpluses, and agricultural products were the heart of Hungary's exports.

As a result, GDP consumed in 1986 was almost 2 percent higher than GDP produced. The trade account ran a deficit, the current accounts an even greater one. Hard-currency debt at the end of the year hit a record $8.5 billion, double the amount of hard-currency exports.[60]

Volume indices for the period of 1978–1986 reflect genuine progress against debt. Output rose by 12 percent, and domestic consumption fell somewhat (see Table 6.1). A 41 percent rise in export volume was accompanied by a mere 3 percent increase in import volume. The economy was thus moving toward trade equilibrium despite a 13 percent deterioration in the terms of trade.

But the data point to some problem areas as well. Many accidental factors can cause a decline in the terms of trade, but an extended, systematic deterioration points to structural problems and an inability to perform in international markets. With these facts in mind, the decline in domestic consumption was bad news at a time when real income grew and total investments fell by as much as 30 percent (investments in fixed assets fell by almost 20 percent). Increased accumulation and investment are the major, if not the sole, prerequisites for structural change—a fact that should be stressed even with the knowledge that stagnant or slowly rising personal consumption was largely responsible

TABLE 6.1
Economic data for 1978–1986[a]

	1984 as Percentage of 1978	1986 as Percentage of 1984	1986 as Percentage of 1978
1. GDP Produced	111.1	100.8	112.0
2. GDP Consumed	95.1	103.6	98.6
3. Gross Investment	68.8	102.3	70.4
4. Of Gross, Investment in Fixed Assets	83.2	97.1	80.8
5. Real Income	106.4	104.9	111.6
6. Real Wages	91.7	102.8	94.3
7. Exports	144.8	97.5	141.2
8. Imports	99.9	102.8	102.8
9. Terms of Trade	91.2	95.5	87.1
Trade surplus/deficit as percentage of GDP[b]			
10. In the First Year	+10.0	−4.0	+10.0
11. In the Last Year of the Period	−4.0	+1.7	+1.7

[a]All are volume indices except for rows 9–11.

[b]A plus sign indicates an import surplus; a minus sign an export surplus.

Source: Statistical Yearbooks of the Hungarian Statistical Office.

for the smooth functioning of the economy and the preservation of social peace.

The indices of personal income show a peculiar duality. Real personal income grew by almost 12 percent while real wages fell by 6 percent, a remarkable percentage difference. Pensions were partly responsible, but the main reason was the growing popularity of second jobs, which enabled families to maintain or increase their consumption levels and living standards.

Dividing these years into two different periods was not arbitrary. In almost every year during the first period, 1978–1984, GDP produced rose, domestic consumption fell, export volume increased, import volume stagnated, and the current-account position improved despite constantly worsening terms of trade. (A declining deficit became a surplus in 1982.) The last year of that period, 1984, was a turning point. In the next two years GDP produced hardly changed, but GDP consumed grew; the volume of exports fell, that of imports rose; the current account was again in deficit, and debt rose to dangerous levels. The policymakers now confronted the problems of the late 1970s all over again, and after eight years, Hungary was not ready to end the consolidation phase.

Changes in the System of Economic Management

Several steps taken in the wake of the policy shift in the late 1970s broke with the existing system of management and pointed anew toward a market economy. In this section I will try to summarize the most important of these measures and their conceptual background. In discussing particular measures, I will try to show how they were integrated into the country's economic system and whether they brought about real change.

The Competitive Price System

After consumer prices had been raised, a reform of producer pricing was on the agenda. The price system introduced on 1 January 1980 was intended to replace cost-plus-profit calculations with prices whose relative values reflected the international marketplace. As the planners saw it, profits and product lines should not depend on manufacturers' ability to raise prices above costs. Rather, the world market should judge how profitable (or loss making) products or companies are at existing cost levels. The goal was to boost exports in a manner consistent with the new policy. The main features of the new system were these:

1. Prices of raw and basic materials and energy would be based on the price of the marginal source—in other words, on the current Western import price converted into forints at the going exchange rate. If the costs of (limited) domestic production or of socialist imports (also limited and converted into forints at the going rate) were much lower than this price, the difference (conceived as rent) would be taxed away. This so-called differential producer tax would finance export subsidies.

2. In manufacturing industries, the base used to establish domestic prices would be the export prices on international markets (that is, their forint equivalents according to the current exchange rate). Firms whose hard-currency exports exceeded 5 percent of their output could not raise their profit rate on domestic and Comecon sales above what was realized on exports to the West, overhead costs being adjusted proportionately. In addition, domestic price movements should follow those of exports. If export prices fell, domestic prices should be lowered accordingly, rising only when export prices rose. This double constraint—equal profitability and parallel price movements—would make price discipline easily enforceable even if market forces were weak. Manufacturers whose hard-currency exports amounted to less than 5 percent of output would apply so-called follower prices; that is, a firm with a similar profile whose domestic prices were export determined would be selected as a "leader," and the "follower" firm would have to follow its lead in pricing.

3. In the noncompetitive sector—services, construction, and construction materials—as well as in agriculture and food processing, prices would continue to be computed on a centrally determined cost-plus-profit basis. Food got special treatment because farm policy throughout Europe, Hungary's main market for agricultural exports, was protectionist, having state subsidies, import quotas, and high tariffs. Domestic prices of processed foods would be based on domestic costs, and competitive products (vegetables, fruits, canned foods, etc.) would be priced according to the market.

The competitive price system outlined under the first two points could, in principle, adapt to changing export and import prices. It was intended that the system would keep producers from exploiting monopolies or shortages and that their low or declining export profitability would be compensated by raising domestic prices. As experts both for and against the system noted, it amounted to a kind of simulative regulation, and it was often argued that the system's success would hinge more on the market developments it triggered than on the quality of the system itself. If at least some import competition were allowed, the system might work. If not, internal inconsistencies would doom it as they had doomed other attempts to regulate prices. The system would be riddled with amendments and then wrecked by bargaining between firms and government.[61]

During the first two years the competitive price system was in effect, the Hungarian economy did not recover. Quite the contrary. In 1982, as we have seen, insolvency was imminent, and even partial liberalization of imports was out of the question. The year 1981 had been one of severe import restrictions, and 1982 and 1983 were even more so. Competition could not take root in the domestic market, and the price system's inherent problems did indeed emerge.

A firm that was able to export efficiently could not risk trying to increase its market share, since the lower prices that would be invoked would cut its domestic prices, too. Temporary export price cuts in a time of recession were tolerable, but not if domestic prices had to be reduced simultaneously. If a firm's export volume were large, it could raise its export efficiency by dropping the least efficient products and thus improve its position before entering a new round of negotiations with the pricing authorities. But under the prevailing conditions, a cut in exports could be harmful. In the end, price bargaining and preferential treatment for particular companies multiplied. Many firms won permission to cut export prices without an equivalent decline in domestic prices as long as their export volume rose. Thus the system fell apart in two or three years, because in the absence of real market forces, it became more and more complex and distorting.

The profitability of exports varies widely, especially in a country whose government meddles in export contracts. Extrapolating such divergent profits to domestic sales is, in the long run, not feasible; attempts to do so would lead to some firms and industries going out of business and others roaring ahead out of all proportion to domestic demand. The government and political leadership were not prepared to accept bankruptcies and plant closings, but they were compelled to slash firms' resources in order to restrain investment. The upshot was that the differentiating effect of the competitive price system was softened through "price rules" and other measures tailored to individual cases. Research has shown that subsidies as well as tax and other exemptions rose after 1980, mainly for firms whose position deteriorated under the new price system. Companies that remained efficient had to contend with higher taxes and shrinking allowances. The government was forced to cut some firms' purchasing power during hard times by abruptly raising tax rates or by instructing the Hungarian National Bank to make unilateral, ex post facto changes in credit contracts and even withdraw outstanding credits. Since you can take only from those who already have something, the profitable firms, those that had some reserves, suffered. The competitive price system could not evolve into a market-based system and became yet another element of indirect economic management.

The Unified Ministry of Industry

As the ideas behind the 1968 reform were revived, there were calls to grant companies more autonomy and to streamline the elaborate system of industrial management. The ministries of heavy industry, metallurgy, engineering, and light industry were merged into a Ministry of Industry with the goal of abolishing direct management of industrial firms by industrial ministries. There was to be an end to the special pleading on the part of the branch ministries; their fights with the Planning Office, Ministry of Finance, and other government agencies; and even the system of subsidies, tax allowances, investment credits, and capital allotments.

The new ministry was to avoid detailed company oversight and deal instead with strategic decision making with regard to large-scale industrial development and the introduction of modern technology. The new ministry retained ownership of the state industrial firms but lacked departments to run those firms. The size of its staff was less than half that of its predecessors.

Soon after the ministry set to work in early 1981, it began to be subjected to conflicting pressures. The government tried to use it in its role as overseer, directing it to instruct companies to increase exports and cut back on imports, distribute import quotas, and arbitrate in disputes between buyers and sellers. Such disputes were common in foreign trade. A textile factory, for example, as seller, would often be interested in exporting directly even if domestic processing by a garment factory could increase the overall volume and profitability of exports. Large companies were glad to fall back on the Ministry of Industry in these disputes; they also sought assistance at the bank, the Ministry of Finance, the Planning Office, the Price Office, and the Labor Office in solving financial problems, rolling over loans, and winning various exemptions and other concessions for their operations.

Since this was a time when selective measures were being taken to cut the firms' purchasing power, which produced hardship and cries for favorable treatment, the Ministry of Industry had its work cut out for it. Successful mediations raised its prestige and brought it new "clients," as other agencies (including the Ministry of Finance and the Price Office) seized the opportunity to deal with individual firms through the new ministry. Within eighteen months, it had taken on all the functions of its predecessors.

New Property Forms of Firms

The measures introduced in 1968 had limited the branch ministries' property rights to companies, and the firms' chief executives had taken on the jobs of enacting and revising company plans and of preserving and enlarging assets. This was a very important principle even if it was not often achieved in practice. The hope was that the unified Ministry of Industry would wean firms from the government.

As experience accumulated and economic theory developed, the problem of the companies' independence turned into a problem of socialist property in general. There were challenges to the fundamental idea behind directed planning, that only the state could act as the trustee of state-owned property. One theme in the literature was that under a system of commodity production, property rights could not in principle be vested in the government save in the case of a few public services. The government's true role was to enact and enforce laws, including laws regulating the economy, and to create new institutions. The state bureaucracy could not assume entrepreneurial risks, but state firms should. It followed that the government should hand over its property rights to business organizations.

Proponents of self-management wanted property rights (or at least a large share of them) vested in the companies themselves. Management would then have the incentives of personal income and investment possibilities to utilize capacity efficiently. The real force for restructuring, however, would be the employees, who would exercise their creativity and thus promote their firms' independence. Once the process began, companies could overcome resistance from government and party bureaucrats facing a loss of power.

Other experts believed that in order to create socialist commodity production, Hungary needed a capital market. And the people who could best allocate capital were not the company managers, whose main interest was to maximize the personal income, including their own, provided by their firms. They were not concerned with seeking out the best investment opportunities in the economy as a whole. The job could only be assumed by business banks that were independent of the central bank or by other institutions set up specially to manage capital. These institutions would have to be kept at arm's length from the bureaucracy, answerable only to the highest authorities—the Parliament or the Presidential Council. With this base, a stock market could be established. By virtue of their jobs (and a suitable incentive system), the staffs of the capital-allocating organizations would have an interest in rational behavior to promote the growth of social capital.[62]

After the threat of insolvency receded, new forms of firm management were in fact introduced, designed to stimulate innovation and make the exercise of property and employer rights more efficient without impairing state property. The years 1985 and 1986 saw property rights in large and medium-sized firms turned over to company councils. These councils were partly elected by the workers, partly chosen by the director from among management. Their charge included matters of organization (decentralization, mergers and breakups, the creation of independent profit centers, etc.) and operations (production plans, development projects, major funding activities, major changes in company activities).

The councils were to ensure the year-end balance, and they hired and fired the CEOs and set their salaries and bonuses. The power to create and liquidate state firms of necessity remained with the ministries and local government councils, but company councils could group together to set up subsidiaries. A CEO was personally responsible for the management of a firm within the guidelines set by the council's decisions. (In companies with a work force of less than 300, a general assembly or assembly of delegates elected by individual departments took the place of these councils.)

The government thus opted for the first of the two proposals sketched above. The most popular argument against the second course, though not necessarily the most convincing, was that banks and other capital-allocating institutions, as heirs to middle-level bureaucrats, would wind up acting according to old habits and in the process become extensions of the state. This was a superficial fear, and basically, politicians were less than sympathetic to steps that would entrench capitalism in a socialist state.[63] Neither the politicians nor the experts probably understood the full import of capital-allocating institutions for socialist commodity production in Hungary.

Some state firms—public utilities and companies in the defense sector—remained under government administration, but most had a new form of management by 1986. Reports (which will not be detailed here) suggest little enthusiasm for the changeover. Workers have accused party and union activists of working jointly to manipulate council and assembly elections, and it is also said that CEO nominations have been manipulated. There is a feeling that the members of the councils are not truly representative and that nothing much can be expected of them.

Company managers say it was difficult enough to fulfill the expectations of the market and the government and that the councils have become one more obstacle. Government administrators complain that although it wasn't easy to influence firms in the past, it is even harder now that they no longer hire the CEOs. The councils have that job, and the ministries cannot order them about. In summary, then, although the dramatic reduction in government control was an important step, the new system is still far from perfect.

The Rise of Small Businesses and Second Jobs

Small-scale production has become popular in agriculture. After the second wave of collectivization in 1959–1961, farming in Hungary was not structured according to the Soviet model adopted elsewhere in Eastern Europe. (Poland was another exception; collectivization was not completed, and smallholding still predominated.) The most important difference between the Hungarian and Soviet systems is that a large part of Hungarian farm output is produced by smallholders—among others, members of cooperatives or workers on large state farms—who have household plots. They are free to sell what they do not consume themselves.

The share of small-scale production in the gross agricultural output was two-fifths in the 1960s and one-third in the 1970s and 1980s. As large farms succeeded in adopting industrial mass-production systems, small producers turned increasingly to labor-intensive products, a fact reflected in their high (50 percent) share of the net output. These producers account for most of Hungary's vegetables, 50–60 percent of its fruit, and more than half of its pork.

A well-defined relationship has emerged between the smallholders and the large state and cooperative farms. The large farms are paid to perform basic operations like plowing and planting the small plots. The smallholders buy seed and breeding stock from the large farms and fatten livestock for them. The large farms provide fertilizers and buy the smallholders' output. This integration gives the smallholders some security, though they remain responsive to the market and produce high-quality food.[64]

The country has 1.5 million small farms with enough land (more than 1,500 square meters) to produce for the market. In most cases, some of the small farms' production is in fact marketed; starting in the mid-1970s, a growing number of smallholders began taking a more professional approach to the business by consuming only a negligible part of their output. Even so, small farming is the livelihood of only a tiny minority; for 2.5–2.7 million people, representing almost every walk of life, farming is a second job. (This figure is equivalent to 600,000–650,000 full-time farm workers, more than the total for large-scale agriculture.) Only 20 percent of the small farms are owned by peasant families; 33 percent are owned by workers, 25 percent by pensioners, and 20 percent by professionals. For some 40 percent of all Hungarian families, small-scale farming is more than a marginal source of secondary income.[65]

The large farms are themselves diversed. They operate food-processing factories, construction companies, retail stores, and restaurants. In the big cities many operate ventures totally unrelated to agriculture—manufacturing clothing and computer chips, doing precision engineering work in cooperation with Western firms, building and renovating housing, cleaning offices and apartments, doing exterminating, and more. This type of activity began in the wake of the 1968 reforms, expanded rapidly in the second half of the 1970s, and provided well-paid jobs for some 200,000–250,000 people by the mid-1980s. In some cases the cooperatives launched the businesses to make money and to provide steady employment for their members and their families. In others, entrepreneurs sought a legal framework for their ideas, and in return they give a stipulated part of their profit to the cooperative. These ventures are small or medium-sized and are totally dependent on the marketplace; if they are not profitable, they go out of business.

Other small businesses have emerged as well, partly because of a decision that the authorities, generally local councils, could not deny trade licenses to applicants meeting the relevant requirements—in the case of a butcher shop, for example, passing a sanitary inspection. (Previously, the officials could decide whether or not a proposed venture was "necessary.") At the same time, the operation of many state shops and restaurants has been contracted out to entrepreneurs, who pay the state a fixed fee or a share of the profits. The number of full-time, pensioner, and part-time (but licensed) crafts people grew between 1975 and 1985 from 84,000 to 150,000, and the number of private shops and restaurants rose from 10,000 to 29,000. Unmet demand means that there are many unlicensed (and rather incompetent) entrepreneurs as well.[66]

As part of the reform package, the government authorized new types of small business in 1981. The goal was to help blue- and white-collar workers in the large state companies find legal, or at least organized, second jobs and thus contribute to the supply of goods and services. Among the new businesses, which began appearing in 1982, three forms are particularly popular.

One is the so-called small cooperative, the membership of which is limited to 100 by the 1981 decree. Their accounting is simplified, and they receive tax breaks, paying only a straight tax on gross income—a boon to the efficient even if the rate is high. Profitable small cooperatives have no cap on members' incomes. They receive credit on favorable terms, and their limited liability (which excludes personal property) offers members more security than would other private ventures. Early on, a number of existing cooperatives with fewer than 100 members adopted the new form; new cooperatives and more reorganizations of old ones followed. Their numbers grew from 200 in 1982 to 10,000 at the end of 1986, mostly in engineering, light industry, and construction, with a total membership of 40,000. Most members have their full-time job with the small cooperative.

The business work partnership (BWP) was established as an autonomous business providing second jobs for no more than 30 people. Members must notify their regular employers that they are participating—a formality, since consent cannot be withheld. BWPs have been set up in diverse industries. Some produce patented equipment on their own machines, and others operate as language schools, matchmakers, and travel agencies. Many are made up of professionals in such fields as computers and architecture. From almost 5,000 BWPs in 1983, there were 11,000, with more than 70,000 members, at the end of 1986.

The enterprise business work partnership (EBWP) is a BWP created by employees of a state company or some other state institution, such as a university, using equipment and often premises rented from their regular employer. Management's consent is naturally required to set up an EBWP and may be withheld without explanation. (Some specialized groups within large cooperatives are run under similar rules, and this discussion of EBWPs applies to them as well.)

In the beginning, the main argument for EBWPs was that they would put unutilized capacity to work, make better use of employees, and increase supplies and competition in industries, both manufacturing and service, that had no small or medium-sized firms. The underlying idea may have been to transfer the successful agricultural model to state industry, and indeed one slogan referred to EBWPs as the "household farms" of big business.

In practice, EBWPs turned out differently. Most work is done not for the outside market but for the parent firms. In industries where a labor shortage keeps capacity idle, members usually perform the same tasks as during regular working hours. EBWPs quite often carry out special jobs related to the firm's usual activity—for example, high-quality, self-managed work for small-batch manufacturing runs or sophisticated design or assembly work. Still, there are cases of EBWPs taking on tasks unrelated to the company's day-to-day operations, such as participation in investment projects, special experiments, and production of parts that were previously purchased.

Whatever the task, the EBWP and the firm's management negotiate the pay (or, in the case of routine production, the piecework rate) for the EBWP workers. EBWP performance cannot be acknowledged if official norms are not already filled. Crucially, the money paid to EBWPs is treated as production costs for the parent company, not wage costs, and is thus exempt from wage regulations.

EBWPs and management bargain fiercely over performance requirements for official working hours since EBWP hourly wages are some 2.5–3 times higher than regular wages and 50 percent higher than weekend overtime wages. This EBWP rate is more or less equivalent to the hourly wage of skilled workers in private industry, ventures sponsored by cooperative farms, and private weekend construction jobs. EBWP pay ordinarily comes to about half what members earn from their regular work, but some members manage to double their income. In either case, EBWPs are an important source of money for their members.

Members sometimes do EBWP work during their regular working hours or claim part of their regular output as EBWP work, which is of course forbidden. But the EBWPs' success is due mainly to skill, effort, and organization. They recruit from the cream of a company's staff, and since wages are regulated, companies themselves often act to start EBWPs, realizing that this is the only way they can offer elite workers an incentive to increase output.

The EBWPs and the specialized groups have grown spectacularly. There were more than 10,000 at the end of 1983; the figure doubled the next year and had reached 21,000 by the end of 1987. At that time, 60 percent of the large industrial firms, 80 percent of the construction companies, and 20 percent of the agricultural firms had such "intrapreneurial" groups. Almost 15 percent of the employees of state industrial firms belonged to an EBWP at their workplace, and the membership had reached 270,000.

There is general agreement that if wages were decontrolled, these groups would be unnecessary. Beyond that, they are the subject of a lively debate. Some observers priase the EBWPs' productivity and sophisticated self-management. Others denounce them as ways of getting around wage regulations and argue that the high EBWP pay devalues regular work and is thus demoralizing. Management has sometimes blocked the formation of EBWPs and specialized groups on these grounds.

Calls to abolish the EBWPs and specialized groups have not attracted much support, however. Firms cannot get along without their output, and in an era of declining real wages, nearly 300,000 people cannot be deprived of the chance to make some extra money. There have been attempts to constrain the organizations—in 1987 a 20 percent tax was introduced on payments to EBWPs—but they have had little effect.

It should be evident by now that Hungary has a dual economy. It is dominated by large state and cooperative firms that operate in an environment of strong, individualized regulation. There is also a large sector of small organizations whose activities are regulated by a somewhat distorted market. This sector may be thought of as Hungary's market sector or its sector of small and medium-sized businesses. It produces goods and offers services that are not profitable for large companies and is organized along different lines. This sector allows businesses to manage their work forces (and, to a limited extent, their capital) relatively freely. By the mid-1980s, an estimated 4 million people, representing two-thirds to three-fourths of Hungary's families, were involved in small business— the equivalent of 1.4 million full-time workers—and the sector produced one-fourth of the country's GDP.

Leaving aside small-scale farm production, 1.1 million people were employed in small organizations in the middle of the 1980s, 700,000 of them part-time, the equivalent of 750,000 full-time workers. The output of the small industrial organizations was 20–25 percent that of state industry; in construction, the figure was 75 percent.[67]

In the 1980s these small organizations increased mainly outside of agriculture, in industry and services. The introduction of new types of small business has given 500,000 people second jobs, which, more than rising pensions and other social benefits, is the reason real income and personal consumption grew between 1978 and 1986 despite a drop in real wages. In other words, rising personal consumption was owing to a longer workday. There are reports of people quite literally making themselves sick by overworking, and, in fact, mortality in men over forty has risen, and the life expectancy of the average male has steadily fallen since the mid-1970s.

The small-business sector undeniably plays a major and—in conformance with official plans—a growing role despite the restrictions imposed on it. Some of these are obvious: legal constraints (limits on the number of employees in some types of small business); progressive, sometimes prohibitive, and often changing taxes; uncertainties in supply; the extremely bad state of the infrastructure (telephone service, for example); and a lack of protection in dealing with larger organizations as buyers and sellers.

There are more subtle problems as well. Official attitudes toward small business are still somewhat ambivalent. Government as yet provides insufficient support despite proclamations that small business should be an integral part of the socialist economy. Small businesses, for their part, have not united effectively to press their interests with the tax authorities and others in the government.

All these difficulties naturally affect the behavior of the people who work in the sector. They tend to downplay their activity and keep their investment plans to themselves, mindful that the political, legal, or administrative climate might worsen. They keep one foot in the socialist sector and pursue their own business only as a sideline, even if they find the latter more satisfying financially and emotionally. If they do give up their regular jobs, they prefer that some family member continue working full-time for a state firm. This part-time mentality weakens competition among small ventures; markets for individual products are fragmented, and monopolies arise even when there are many potential suppliers of a given product.[68] Despite these generally discouraging notes, a few small ventures are steadily—sometimes illegally—piling up capital.

Changes in the Banking System Toward a Bond Market

Before the 1980s, Hungary's banking system was characterized by both a separation of functions and a complete monopoly. The Hungarian National Bank (HNB), the chief issuing bank, was also a business bank, supplying short-, medium-, and long-term credits and accepting deposits from businesses. The HNB had a monopoly on credit—companies were not allowed to grant each other commercial credits—and only the HNB could hold foreign exchange—companies and individuals had to exchange their foreign currency there. Only the National Savings Bank (NSB) and associated savings cooperatives could accept deposits from individuals, and the NSB also served as the business bank for small firms. The State Development Bank financed investments out of the state budget, and insurance policies were handled by the State Insurance Company.

This overcentralization was under attack as the 1968 reform was being planned, but that reform left the structure of the banking sector unchanged. To tell the truth, the sector's structure and division of labor, inherited from the era of directed planning, proved adequate for the needs of the indirect system of management established in the 1970s. Only a bank with a strong monopoly on credit could enforce investment restrictions while manipulating the financial standing of individual firms in accordance with central directives.

Interestingly, this system came under attack from the government's own Science Committee, which proposed the creation of funds, separate from the government budget, to finance innovation (on sound banking principles, to be sure). The existing innovation fund was depleted, and it was thought that banklike management of such money would be more productive. The result was the establishment, from 1981 to 1986, of ten small banks, one of which was set up specifically to promote foreign trade. There were also two joint-venture banks in Budapest, using both Hungarian and foreign capital, and two Hungarian banks operating in the West (Vienna and London).

The lending decisions of these small banks are not under the control of the government or any other central authority. They lend according to financial criteria and have their own investments, including risk-capital operations. Oddly enough, they owe their existence to the shortage of central resources and investment opportunities; at the time they were created, the only way to finance small but viable investment projects was to ease restrictions on capital.

The small banks have little capital and thus limited influence on capital allocation in the economy as a whole. They do not offer much competition to the bigger lenders, but they are still in existence, learning the business, seeking their proper place in the Hungarian economy, and expanding their range of activities. They have had successes and failures, but however slowly, the monolithic banking system is eroding.

That erosion is not limited to the financing of innovation. Since 1983 firms and other public institutions, such as local councils and the Post Office, have been allowed to raise capital by issuing bonds. In general, only firms may hold these bonds, though the Ministry of Finance may authorize bond issues intended for the general public. The state backs these bonds as lender of last resort, thus demolishing the monopoly of the National Savings Bank and its associated cooperatives. As the bonds pay more interest than do NSB deposits, there is a brisk popular demand for them, and a bond market has emerged. The bonds' importance should not be overestimated, however. The total value of bonds in circulation in 1986 was 8 billion forints, of which individuals held 6 billion forint. In the same year, investment outlays and individual NSB deposits combined came to more than 250 billion forints.

The State Insurance Company was split into two competing firms in 1986, and on 1 January 1987 there was a truly major change: The HNB became an issuing bank, with its business-banking functions turned over to new large banks spun off from it. These banks are in their infancy; they have little capital, and refinancing from the HNB is for the moment very limited.

*   *   *

Still other changes in the economic system were made during the 1980s. It is not possible to list them all, but three in particular should be mentioned. First, several measures were taken to attract and protect foreign investments; and second, there were some steps in 1985 to liberalize wage regulations (these led to large wage increases and were quickly repealed). Third, a bankruptcy law was introduced in 1986 (to give it the official name, a "procedure to be followed in case of liquidation and reorganization"). Any economic unit dealing with an ailing state firm, cooperative, or registered small business, as well as the ailing business itself, could initiate bankruptcy action in court. This was a change from the previous policy, according to which the government had to step in if a firm went bankrupt.

All of these changes pointed in the direction of a market economy, but they have had only a small effect for several reasons, lack of groundwork and half-heartedness among them. Other factors have had more of a role in shaping economic decisions.

Functioning of the Economy

After 1978, the following goals guided economic policymakers: improving the hard-currency balance of trade, reducing the debt, and avoiding internal strife. Case-by-case regulation was used to increase exports and restrict imports. The government struck deals with manufacturing and foreign-trade companies that allowed so much in the form of bonuses, wage increases, and extra import allowances in return for a certain amount of additional hard-currency exports or cuts in imports. Import quotas were reduced, and import licensing was tightened. As we have seen, extra exports could mean a firm would receive permission to raise domestic prices.

Bent on averting conflict, the leadership would not allow the liquidation of weak firms. Unable to face the social and political dilemma of structural unemployment, full employment was maintained. There was some economic justification for this policy. Since opportunities to import were limited, a decline in domestic production would cause domestic shortages and thus affect businesses' ability to obtain inputs and endanger export commitments (including government-level Comecon contract commitments). Preserving manufacturing capacity meant increasing amounts of aid, through a variety of allowances and subsidies, to weak firms. The value of transfers to ailing businesses during the 1980s has been estimated at almost 20 percent of GDP.

If a foreign-trade equilibrium were to be created, domestic consumption had to shrink. Since personal consumption had to be kept stable to avoid unrest, the burden fell on investment. Firm-level investment funds were constantly reduced, even though this action meant taking away an increasing share of the firms' income. The strong preference for exports and the help given to exporting firms created extra income but endangered the hard-won equilibrium. Trade problems multiplied: The terms of trade worsened every year while interest and principal payments on Hungary's debt grew. More and more purchasing power had to be withdrawn from the domestic market.

Policymakers were forced to apply the brakes, but since the leadership wanted to avoid bankruptcies, monetary measures were out of the question—raising interest rates, devaluing the forint, and restricting credit. These measures would have affected everyone equally, with selective results: The weak would have gone bankrupt. The government turned instead to fiscal measures, mainly changes in the tax system. Tax rates were raised almost yearly, subsidies and tax allowances were changed constantly, new taxes were introduced, and at times the entire system was overhauled. The rules on company reserve funds were changed. The funds were increased and spending controls were tightened until 80 percent of an average firm's profit was set aside in this way.

Overall, the 1980s saw the emergence of an even less transparent indirect system of macroeconomic management in which (1) export incentives and import restrictions, specified in yearly contracts between the government and individual firms, were widespread; (2) price, wage, and credit regulations were used to influence the fortunes of individual firms; and (3) the tax system (including subsidies and allowances) was used to achieve a general contraction.

This system was intended to be only temporary during the consolidation phase. Consolidation, however, lasted until the end of the decade with no end in sight, which was damaging in several ways. Investment opportunities dried up, and modernization was postponed even in factories that produced and exported efficiently. Machinery also deteriorated. The situation was not helped by the fact that a large part of the investments that were made were directed to large, ailing firms. Table 6.2 sums up the state of affairs in the mid-1980s.

The volume of investment in industry had grown despite the decline in total investment, and inefficient mining investments had grown more than twofold. Investment in metallurgy, an industry in crisis, had fallen by nearly 10 percent, but investment in the main exporting sectors—engineering and light industry—had dropped by almost one-fourth and

TABLE 6.2
Increases in investment volume, 1975–1985 (1975=100)

Total Investments	95.9
Total Investments in Industry	105.0
Mining	216.5
Electricity	153.8
Metallurgy	91.9
Engineering	78.6
Light Industry	53.5

Source: *Statistical Yearbooks* of the Hungarian Statistical Office.

one-half, respectively. Mining, electricity, and metallurgy investments had accounted for only 36 percent of total investment between 1976 and 1980, but their combined share rose to 46 percent in the early 1980s.[69]

With the general contraction, everyone lost income—strong, healthy firms included. Developed and the more advanced developing countries, meanwhile, were growing rapidly because of new electronics-based technologies and radical structural changes that favored small companies. At the same time, Hungary's structural backwardness was becoming chronic. Imports were uncertain, even when they were necessary for production, which was a major problem for a small country like Hungary. Forced import substitution led to problems with quality, and export markets were lost.[70]

This environment had its effect on the behavior of individuals and businesses. The forced setting aside of 80 percent of profits hurt firms, and the constant, unpredictable changes in regulations made every calculation uncertain. A project that looked profitable might lose money if the rules were changed. There was less and less incentive to grasp market opportunities, since if a promising initiative lost money at the outset a firm's hard-currency import quota would be cut. The government taxed everything it could find. It did not pay to pursue excellence.

Disagreements within the government made the climate even more unstable. After 1982, with the threat of insolvency overcome, the leadership proclaimed the need for "more dynamic growth." Macroeconomic planning is always prone to optimism, and the yearly plans were now built on forecasts of domestic resources and foreign-trade opportunities that left almost nothing for reserves. When the forecasts proved wrong, new restrictive measures were required to preserve equilibrium.

It would be an exaggeration to say that no large Hungarian companies were truly successful in the 1980s (other than in bureaucratic bargaining), but in general, deteriorating conditions, fast-changing regulations, and companies' behavior fed on each other and promoted stagnation. It seemed, as the data above suggest, that the economy had reached its limits under the prevailing conditions. The year 1984 was comparatively successful, but 1985–1986 saw the debt problem deepen and economic performance, measured in constant prices, barely improve. The first half of 1987 offered no relief.

Economic policy in the decade of stagnation cannot be called a complete failure. In 1978, domestic consumption surpassed GDP realized by 10 percent. Within three to four years, Hungary stabilized its debt, then cut it. This task was immense, almost unprecedented, and achieved without serious social tension, but it exhausted the country's reserves. Hungary fell further behind the rest of the world. The system of indirect economic management, having gone as far as it could, became a caricature of itself. Companies grew less autonomous than they had been even in the 1970s, and they grew less innovative.

The weakness and eventual failure of the reform measures, the growing dependence of firms on government, and the economic stagnation affected all of Hungarian society. The leadership lost its credibility, and the people grew cynical. The situation cried out for change.[71]

7

Toward a Breakthrough?
(1987–1988)

The situation in Hungary in 1987 and 1988 can be outlined only by relying on a great number of actual facts, especially since the processes were speeding up at that time and people realized—the author being no exception—that they represented a groping toward an uncertain future. For these reasons, this chapter contains many details and has a rather peculiar structure. In the first section, I present one political event, the May 1988 conference of the Hungarian Socialist Workers' party, and then try to give a sketch of the hectic political and economic life of the country at the time through a mosaic of news from the daily press. In the last three sections, I try to present a more systematic picture of the political and economic processes of 1987 and 1988.

Changes at the Top

May of 1988 was a breakthrough in a sense. It was a surprise in itself that the Hungarian Socialist Workers' party convened a party conference for 21 May, because between two party congresses, only a so-called mid-point Central Committee session is customary. (The last congress had been held in 1985, and the next one was due in 1990.) Delegates to the party conference were not elected according to the old elector system; instead, every 1,000 party members could send a representative. The conference also assumed the role of a congress (a situation previously unheard of) in that it included in its agenda the reelection of the Central Committee (a kind of party parliament) and of the Political Committee (the ten–fifteen-member topmost organ of the party). (The Communist party of the Soviet Union also held a party conference in June 1988, under the auspices of speeding up *glasnost* and *perestroika,* but that conference did not elect new central bodies.)

Speeches during the two-day-long conference were rather sharp. The majority of the speakers presented a gloomy picture of the present, criticized the many faults and errors that had been committed and the indecisiveness of the leadership, and demanded determined, radical reform steps. The remarks were no longer limited to the economy; they also pertained to the political reform and the radical realignment of political structures.

Everyone was shocked by the new composition of the leading party organs that resulted. It was strange in itself that one-third of the Central Committee members changed, although the need for such a change had been raised even before the conference and the list of candidates had been drawn up accordingly. What was shocking was the fact that five members of the previous thirteen-member Political Committee, all of them old and trusted Kádár cronies, were not even reelected to the Central Committee (CC), which made it impossible for them to remain on the Political Committee (PC). The five who did not obtain 50 percent of the votes, and were therefore defeated, were as follows: Sándor Gáspár, general secretary of the Trade Union Center (TUC) and president of the World Trade Union Alliance (71, CC member since 1956, PC member since 1962); Ferenc Havasi, first secretary of the Budapest party committee and until 1987 secretary for economic affairs of the CC (59, CC member since 1966, PC member since 1980); György Lázár, prime minister from 1975 until 1987 and then the deputy of the party's general secretary, i.e., Kádár (64, CC member since 1970, PC member since 1975); Károly Németh, president of the Presidential Council, previously deputy of the party's general secretary (66, CC member since 1957, PC member since 1970); and Miklós Óvári, the most intimate colleague of Kádár and rumor has it, a coauthor of his speeches and articles (63, CC member since 1966, PC member since 1975). János Kádár (75) was elected party chairman, a highly ceremonial function.

Károly Grósz (58), who for years had been considered as a possible heir to Kádár and who had become prime minister in 1987, was the new general secretary. Of the eleven members of the new Political Committee, six were totally new members, two had served one year, and three had served three years. Two outspoken reform politicians were elected to the Political Committee: Rezsö Nyers and Imre Pozsgay. Nyers (65) had been secretary for economic affairs of the Central Committee from 1963 until 1974. He had been the leading politician responsible for the preparation, introduction, and further development of the economic reform; in the period when the reform was halted, he had been stripped of this function and had also lost his Political Committee membership, although he had remained as a member of the Central Committee; later he had worked first as director then as scientific adviser at the Institute of Economics of the Hungarian Academy of Sciences and was an éminence grise of the reform wing both inside and outside the party. Imre Pozsgay (55) is a teacher by profession. He had been elected to the Central Committee in 1980 and was known to be a politician who had strong contacts with the semilegal opposition and social scientists who criticized the political structure and devised measures for its reform. He had often turned up at meetings of these people and had given voice in other ways also to his radical political inclinations. In March and April of 1988, the news had spread that because of his views, he would be stripped of his position as general secretary of the Patriotic People's Front and "sent to the countryside" as first secretary of a county council of the party.

The May 1988 conference was a breakthrough in the sense that it ended the almost thirty-year-long autocracy of the Kádár leadership within the party. New faces emerged in the highest governing body of the party and among them were two well-known reform politicians who formerly, both in party circles and publicly, had distanced themselves from the Kádárian center and in many respects had opposed it.

News from the Hungarian Press

In this section, I try to give a multifaceted impression of the actual state of Hungarian society after the May 1988 party conference. The extracts are mostly from two newspapers, *Népszabadság,* the official daily of the Hungarian Socialist Workers' party, and *Heti Világgazdaság* (HVG for short), the very popular weekly of the Hungarian Chamber of Commerce. The time period spanned is from the beginning of June 1988 until the end of November 1988. I have chosen only items that deal with economics and domestic politics. Even if pertaining to domestic politics, I have left out news items about corruption, but here I should mention that in the more open atmosphere of the postconference period obscure property deals and other kinds of abuse of power on the part of lower-level government and party functionaries were made public and brought to court.

The excerpts throw light on new political developments that accelerated so dramatically after the party congress and also illustrate certain dramatic new events that took place within the economy. Moreover, these news reports provide information on facts and problems that previously had been considered secret, and thus inappropriate for public discourse; in the more liberal atmosphere after the party conference, they were put before the public by the Fourth Estate, with new exhilaration. (Translation is by the author.)

Demonstrations

Some 2,000 people held a peaceful demonstration in Kiskőrös demanding government action to improve the dismal state of wine sales. . . . The demonstration of the farmers broke up peacefully Tuesday in the late hours (no policemen in uniform were seen on the spot). (*HVG*, 18 June 1988, pp. 53–54)

Yesterday evening several groups organized a peaceful demonstration in Budapest. The 25,000–30,000 participants gathered at the Square of Heroes. They listened to a warning and a memorandum protesting against the planned destroying by Romania of historic buildings and relics that are considered part of Europe's cultural heritage. (*Népszabadság*, 28 June 1988, p. 4)

Students of the Faculty of Humanities of the Attila József University in Szeged yesterday held a one-day warning strike as a by-product of a debate on reforming higher education. . . . They demanded in a declaration total autonomy for graduate-level education in choosing curricula and other matters of substance. . . . Obligatory ideological subjects should be replaced by subjects chosen by the faculty from the realm of social sciences and the history of philosophy. Marxism and Russian language should be optional, not compulsory. The declaration was sent to government organs, the Parliament, to social organizations, to other universities and colleges, and to the press. (*Népszabadság*, 29 September 1988, p. 6)

The mass demonstration organized in Budapest on 22 November as a commemoration of the Brasov upheaval of last year was dispersed by the police. The twenty-one independent organizations supporting the demonstration intended to march with placards before the Romanian embassy. In several cities all over the world Romanian Days were held on the same day. . . . The demonstration was registered with the police on the ninth of November but on the eleventh the answer was given that neither the meeting nor the march may be held. (*HVG*, 26 November 1988, p. 11)

Against the Danube Dam and Power Plant and Environmental Pollution

On 27 May, many thousands of people gathered in Budapest to demonstrate against the construction of the Bős-Nagymaros Dam and the Austrian participation in it. The crowd gathering on Vörösmarty Square was addressed by the biologist János Vargha, the representative of the Danube Circle. He demanded that the construction be halted, the contracts with the Austrian firms annulled, and the environmental effects of the construction openly debated in the press, radio, and television. (*HVG*, 4 June 1988, p. 9) [A whole complex of dams and power plants is envisaged under an intergovernmental Czechoslovak-Hungarian contract on the Danube between

Bratislava and Budapest. Some of the experts are for the investment, some of them—mainly environmentalists—are against, due to unforeseeable environmental effects, high investment costs, and dubious efficiency. *G. R.*]

[The American-Hungarian Environment Protection Fund, created in 1987 to fight against the Bös-Nagymaros Power Plant, wrote an open letter on 20 January 1988 to the president of the Hungarian Presidential Council. The letter raises several environmental and efficiency issues arguing against the construction of the hydroelectric station. The letter puts the total cost of the core investment, plus environmental and settlement protection measures at $2.2 billion, i.e., 110 billion forints. Of this, $0.5 billion is the Austrian loan. The letter closes with the words:] We the undersigned humbly request the Presidential Council to . . . open a public debate over the Bös-Nagymaros Dam, thus sharing the burden of this historic decision with Hungarian society. (*HVG,* 16 July 1988, p. 53)

[János Szentágothai, the former president of the Hungarian Academy of Sciences (HAS), on the Danube dam:] The intergovernmental contract was signed in 1977. I got wind of it only in 1981 (I certainly knew there was such a plan in the fifties). . . . At the request of György Aczél, the presidency of the HAS dealt with the problem and declared at its 20 December 1983 session that the concept was totally wrong. We suggested that the government cancel the plan or at least defer it for a long period. The 20 December resolution, whose source materials were at that time "highly confidential," "for official use only," has been forwarded to the government by the presidency of the HAS. (*HVG,* 1 October 1988, p. 5)

Before the debate over the government communiqué on the *Bös-Nagymaros investment,* MPs obtained a report of the Hungarian Academy of Sciences with the ministry's comments. Nineteen MPs asked permission to speak. . . . After the reply of László Maróthy, minister of environmental and water management, Parliament accepted with 317 notes (19 against, 31 abstentions) the government's communiqué and the oral supplement, adding that the fulfillment of environmental protection, water purification, and resettlement tasks must be ensured. (*Parliamentary Reports,* October 1988)

New Political Movements and Organizations

Last Saturday, on the first anniversary of the famous Laki-telek meeting, a new political-ideological movement, an independent social organization, was announced under the name Hungarian Democratic Forum (HDF). The caucus, which had 370 participants, adopted a charter and a foundation letter. . . . [Excerpts:] HDF is an independent political-ideological movement embracing not only the entire country but every Hungarian wherever he or she lives. . . . The movement has to develop on its own. It does not accept the labels and constraints of either progovernment or opposition.

Although the HDF deems it necessary to create sooner or later a multiparty system, under present circumstances it does not intend to organize itself as a party but wants to preserve its coalition movement character, open to every honest Hungarian idea and initiative. (*HVG*, 10 September 1988, p. 7)

A group of leading Hungarian intellectuals—writers, sociologists, economists, journalists—created in December 1987 an organization called the New March Front. Their aim is to discuss the most important actual problems of society and to work out plans, suggestions, standpoints. They try to aid in this way the denouement of the crisis. As a basis of their activity they accept socialism and its improvement by reforms. They will not create a political organization. (*Népszabadság*, 17 September 1988, p. 5) [The New March Front could publish its declaration, adopted in March 1988 and signed by nineteen well-known intellectuals, only in mid-September. G. R.]

Under the title *Small Hungarian Politography*, the journal presents a list of alternative organizations as of 4 November. Listed are the name of the organization, date of foundation, number of adherents or sympathizers, the goal and activity of the organization. *Society of Followers of Bajcsy Zsilinszky:* 6 June 1986; 500 members; to create a coalition between the reform wing of the HSWP [Hungarian Socialist Workers' party] and the alternative organizations. *Leftwing Alternative Association:* fall of 1988; 300 members; rejects both the Stalinist and the bourgeois course, tries to establish a self-governing society along the lines of the Liska model. *Danube Circle:* 1984; members come and go; environmental protection, first of all in the Danube Valley. *League of Young Democrats:* 30 March 1988; 1,600 members; the representation of the political will of its member groups and individual members. *Hungarian Democratic Forum:* 3 September 1988; 6,000–7,000 members; alternative proposals for local, national, and international issues, political actions, possibly transformation into a party. *Democratic Movie Union:* 4 October 1988; 400 members; the defense of the interests of film, television, and video markets; the union is independent of the TUC. *Nagymaros Committee:* June 1988; nineteen environmentalist groups; to review the concept of the Bös-Nagymaros investment, do away with secrecy surrounding the construction. *Openness Club National Society:* 29 October 1988; 450 members; oppose methods, procedures contradicting openness. *Quay Club:* fall 1982; 1,500 participants; lectures, debates on neglected topics of history and present-day politics. *Republican Circle:* 27 April 1988; 200 members; debating society taking position on actual social and political problems, cooperating with other autonomous movements. *Network of Free Initiatives:* 1 May 1988; 1,500 members ; to have it accepted that legalized opposition is a basic institution of every democracy; it endorses the self-organization of civil society, independent of the state. *Democratic Union of Scientific Workers:* 14 May 1988; 2,500 members;

defends the interests of those working in science; is independent of the TUC. *New March Front:* 1988; no members, only participants; to reform the political institutional system, to increase the role of groupings of the citizens, to reassess the history of the recent past. *Péter Veres Society:* spring 1987; 1,500–2,000 members; to cherish the memory of Péter Veres, is engaged in the problems of the Hungarian countryside; they have not yet decided whether a party representing the peasantry and the countryside is necessary or not. (*HVG,* 12 November 1988, p. 51)

Today a new political organization was formed in Jurta Theater with 998 members under the name League of Free Democrats. [Excerpt from the program statement and preliminary statute of LFD] LFD tries to influence political decisions on the local and national level, it endorses and criticizes candidates in elections and may suggest its own candidates. (*HVG,* 19 November 1988, p. 9)

Legal Developments

[Excerpts from the address of Imre Pozsgay to Parliament:] The government suggests to Parliament that it discuss at its December session the draft bills on associations, demonstrations, and strikes . . . at its 1989 first term sessions the concept of rewriting the constitution and the modification of the law on courts . . . and also the draft bill on information, which incorporates the principle of the freedom of the press. The modification of the law on elections is also due in the first half of next year. . . . There is no obstacle to enacting laws guaranteeing human rights before the new constitution becomes law. In a legal state—which is our goal—the constitution has to conform to norms on human rights and not vice versa. . . . As we see it now, a new constitution has to be worked out in this parliamentary cycle, probably in 1990. . . ." In his reply to comments, Imre Pozsgay agreed with those who openly requested a multiparty system. He said in this respect that when the first buds of multiparty system not contradicting the constitution will be visible, society will create its parties, not the government. (*Parliamentary Reports,* November 1988)

Foreign Debt, Foreign Investment

The Hungarian National Bank signed a $200-million credit contract with a consortium of thirty-one banks. . . . The organizers of the loan were the Arab Banking Corporation, Bank of Tokyo, Creditanstalt-Bankverein, Dai-Ichi Kangyo Bank, Deutsche Bank A.G., First National Bank of Chicago, and Industrial Bank of Japan. (*HVG,* 11 June 1988, p. 7)

The Hungarian National Bank will issue in Frankfurt bonds worth 200 million DM. The agreement was reached last week between the representatives of the HNB and a twenty-one-strong organizing group led by the Deutsche Bank. (*HVG,* 2 July 1988, p. 6)

[Excerpt from a protocol:] On 12 May 1988, the House of Representatives of the U.S. Congress rejected after a three-hour debate the proposal that OPIC [Overseas Private Investment Corporation], the government institution assisting U.S. foreign investments, extend its activity to Hungary. (*HVG,* 25 June 1988, p. 512)

[Excerpt from the address of Miklós Németh to the session of the Central Committee of the HSWP:] For years the weakest point of the Hungarian economy, threatened with crisis, has been the balance of the current account. We have to pay yearly 65–70 percent of our export receipts from the convertible currency area on interest and principle, and this cannot be accomplished without drawing new foreign credits. In three years, 1984–1987, debt to the Western countries doubled, efficiency deteriorated, the national income decreased if one takes into account the worsening of the terms of trade. In 1987 some positive signs emerged, but they are enough only to slow the negative tendencies, not to reverse them. (*Népszabadság,* 14 July 1988, pp. 1–2)

The Hungarian National Bank devalued on 19 July the forint by 6 percent relative to convertible currencies. (*HVG,* 23 July 1988, p. 5)

At present there are 200 registered joint ventures in Hungary. Not all of them are functioning, however, as generally two years elapse from foundation to production; thus, time is needed to carry out investments. There invariably is a strong interest in starting ventures; three to four new firms are created every week. Capital inflow up to now is about $200 million. (*Népszabadság,* 27 August 1988, p. 4)

Vienna will in the future be better prepared to receive the flood of Hungarian shopping tourists—said Hans Mayr, the vice mayor of the Austrian capital, on Tuesday. As Mayr told us, on 7 November, which was a Monday but a holiday in Hungary, Vienna had a hundred thousand Hungarian visitors who spent at least half a billion schillings. The "Hungarian rush" is good news for Austrian economy and trade but caused serious traffic peoblems. (*Népszabadság,* 9 November 1988, p. 9)

Sándor Demján, chairman and CEO of Magyar Hitelbank Rt., signed in the Hotel Hilton a joint-venture deal with Kim Woo Choong, the president of the South Korean Daewoo group. . . . The total capital of the two joint ventures established by the treaty is $190 million. . . . The South Korean share in both ventures is 50 percent. A letter of intent was also signed whereby a joint venture making car accessories, later assembling whole cars, will also be established. (*Népszabadság,* 22 November 1988, p. 5)

Subsidies, Taxes, Inflation

After 1 July, the coal mining industry's government subsidy will be reduced by 1 billion forints, and after next year, the industry will be stripped of the whole 6 billion forints by which it has been annually subsidized to finance its current deficits—Péter Medgyessy, deputy prime minister, said last week. (*HVG,* 18 June 1988, p. 7)

A four-year subsidy reduction program was developed in order to decrease the present 215-billion-forint government subsidy to production and consumption to 82 billion forints by 1993—we were told at the press conference after the session of the Economic Committee. Although central management has declared several times its intention to reduce subsidies, they grew threefold between 1980 and 1988, and producer subsidies grew by 50 percent. . . . To reduce subsidies—an indispensable element of a liberalization program—meets with obstacles as it cannot be implemented without raising prices and charges. [Of the 75-billion-forint consumer price subsidy, 20 billion forints go to household energy, 13 billion to local transport, 5 billion to milk and milk products, 7 billion to drinking water and canalization, 16 billion to medicine, and 11 billion to the maintenance of council flats.] (*HVG,* 5 November 1988, p. 69)

At the end of this year there will be a one-week heating-lighting restriction on the Lóránd Eötvös University. The cause is that this year's budget of the institution is 30 million forints less than last year's. Besides saving measures, the university has tried to ease tensions . . . by business ventures. . . . Lately they organized Hungarian language courses for the 300 Chinese guest workers of Rába factory. (*Népszabadság,* 12 November 1988, p. 11)

The leaders of the Confederation of Entrepreneurs sent an open letter to MPs demanding a reduction of entrepreneurial and personal income taxes. (*HVG,* 27 August 1988, p. 54)

"Considering the state of the Hungarian economy, it is indispensable to raise corporate taxes" . . . said Péter Medgyessy, deputy prime minister, yesterday at the meeting of the presidium of the Hungarian Economic Society. . . . "The government is aware of the risks of the chosen economic policy. First of all, inflation may speed up owing to wage and import liberalization. The latter is also in close relation to the forint's exchange rate." In this respect—reacting to the union's claim for a voice of its own—he declared: "Exchange rate policy is not a matter of public consensus. Import liberalization may prompt a change in the exchange rate." (*Népszabadság,* 22 November 1988, p. 5)

The modification of personal income tax brackets due next year was debated by the Parliament's ad hoc committee. . . . According to reports, the Ministry of Finance holds that the "underperformance" of the population is caused not by the tax system but by the rigid wage regulation, which needs rethinking. MPs did not agree with this statement, and every speaker said that the tax is too progressive and that there are too many tax brackets. (*Népszabadság*, 22 November 1988, p. 5)

Later on the Parliament dealt in second reading with the draft bill of entrepreneurial profit taxation. After five comments and the reply of the minister of finance, the Parliament reduced the original 55 percent rate of the tax to 50 percent (from *Parliamentary Reports*, November 1988).

Unemployment, Strikes, Wages

To ease employment problems and to rekindle entrepreneurial spirit, so-called restart loans were made available from July in Baranya, Borsod-Abauj-Zemplén, and Komárom counties. Recipients of such a loan may create—under well-specified conditions—new workplaces for themselves, thus easing the responsibility of the state. . . . Everybody whose labor contract has expired and who has obtained from the local council's labor department an authorization for a prolonged notice period may apply for a loan. (*Népszabadság*, 8 August 1988, p. 5)

In the middle of August, 576 persons were registered as seeking employment at the Labor Exchange of the Ózd City Council. Not all of them are unemployed, however, as 50 have a job but wish to change for a better, 40 have been notified that they will be laid off, 230 have been working—for two months—on public works. (*Népszabadság*, 29 August 1988, p. 6)

A blueprint for unemployment benefit. In the last two years the number of unemployed who turned to the official Labor Exchange steadily grew. There were 16,000 this summer. According to official forecasts, their number will further grow and it is not inconceivable that the number will soon run to 100,000. It is no wonder therefore that at the 25 October press conference the government's decision to introduce the unemployment benefit earlier than previously intended (1 January 1989) was announced. (*HVG*, 19 November 1988, p. 50)

For the first time in several decades a much publicized strike broke out on 23 August at the István colliery of the Pécs branch of Mecsek Coal Mines. The firm is one of the three least efficient coal mines, lately very much in the limelight owing to its financial reorganization. . . . The miners found that their paychecks, net of taxes, are 30–40 percent less than they were last year. (*HVG*, 3 September 1988, pp. 4–5)

The recently founded Union of University Teachers demands a onetime 40 percent pay rise in 1989. UUT, which was established—because of infighting among delegates—without a program and regulations in early October, will not leave the Teacher Union or the Trade Union Center. . . . The new representative body of filmmakers however, the Democratic Movie Union, declared independence from the TUC.. (*HVG*, 22 October 1988, p. 8)

Capital Market, Enterprise Reorganization

The National Development Office will invest 540 million forints in the bankrupt Soroksár Foundry, converting part of its debt into stocks. . . . Besides, the Foundry Provision Firm (the "legal predecessor") will take a 150-million-forint share, the Industrial Development Bank an additional 10-million-forint share, in the new firm reorganized as a joint-stock company. . . . The foundry owes 2 billion forints to the state; the bulk of the debt will be reimbursed by the Office of Financial Reorganizations. (*HVG*, 2 July 1988, p. 72)

[An open letter to the minister:] Dear Comrade Marjai! I inform you that our Enterprise Council accepted my suggestion to give autonomy to our factories so that they do not cross-finance one another. I was pressed to make this step because the firm is financially in a critical state; we may go soon in the red, and the banks cannot bail us out, given the restrictive measures of monetary policy. My analysis of the situation led me to the conclusion that a *decisive* part in the coming about of this situation was played by the changing government judgment of socialist, and within that Soviet, exports. I feel obliged to draw your attention, as a person bearing high-level responsibility for this area, to the untenable conditions reigning here. . . . Yours, Ádám Angyal, director general of Ganz Danubius Ship- and Cranebuilding Company. Budapest, 5 July 1988. (*HVG*, 16 July 1988), p. 8)

[From the answer:] Dear Comrade Angyal! . . . Owing to changing world market prices in 1986–1988, our terms of trade with socialist countries improved and very probably will further improve in the coming years. To have a balanced trade, our partners should send us many more goods than originally envisaged, if we on our part stick to our export volume fixed for the next five-year period. As our partners do not have enough goods for our purposes with which to counterbalance the terms-of-trade improvement and as we do not want (we cannot afford) to sell on credit, some curtailment of our export is indispensable . . . we need to reduce first of all the shipment of the least efficient, the most material-intensive products. . . . The tightening of the conditions of ruble export reflects this intent and perception, and this is what is felt by the leadership of Ganz Danubius too. . . . Budapest, 28 July 1988. With comradely greeting, József Marjai. (*HVG*, 6 August 1988, p. 9)

Until the end of this year, the Ganz Danubius Ship- and Cranebuilding Company will be transformed into a group of joint-stock and limited liability firms, under the management of a fifty-person holding company. This is the decision of the company's enterprise council. . . . Ádám Angyal, CEO of the shipbuilding company, says that . . . the disbandment is the only way to save the works after tightening by the government of the terms of socialist export. (*HVG,* 15 October 1988, p. 8)

After having formed at its April general session the securities secretariat, the executive organ of the future stock exchange, the consortium of twenty-five banks and financial institutions interested in the domestic trade of securities last week elected a self-governing body, the Stock Exchange Board. Bit by bit the technical and organizational preconditions of the Hungarian stock exchange are created. . . . A new phenomenon on the securities market is the livelier trade in shares, although this concerns only new issues. In the first six months of 1988 new shares were issued by twenty-one organizations. Among them we find the ten subsidiaries of the recently formed Medicor concern, who issued among themselves securities worth 1.5 billion mrd forints. (*HVG,* 6 August 1988, p. 68)

According to the CEO of Videoton, they intend, as a step toward a market economy, to create this year an intrafirm organization. . . . In this organization, Videoton Electronics Company would be a holding company, having shares in or being the sole owner of its subsidiaries and of a newly formed joint-stock company, Videoton Works Ltd. Thirty percent of the shares of the company, having 10-billion-forint capital, would be floated. (*Népszabadság,* 1 November 1988, p. 3)

The company law was accepted—after some minor amendments—unanimously by Parliament following a statement by Minister of Justice Kálmán Kulcsár, debate, and the minister's answer. (*Parliamentary Reports,* October 1988)

The Political Scene in 1987 and 1988

It is a commonplace that the roots of social-political processes may be found in history and in the thousand manifestations of the life of a society. In previous chapters I hope I have revealed some of the roots of Hungary's economic situation in the late 1980s—those lying in the economic processes of the previous forty years. In trying now to relate the *political* side of the history of 1987 and 1988, I start with two series of events.

By the fall of 1986, the disappointing economic results of 1985–1986 and the failure of the 1984 forced speeding up of economic growth became evident. Leading party and government organs had to face the fact that in 1987—after two milder years—real wages would once again have to be reduced. The Central Committee of the Hungarian Socialist Workers' party was confronted with the new phase of the failure at its 1986 November session, when it dealt with the economic program for 1987. The course of the session is unknown to the public (such debates were made public only at the party conference in May 1988 and afterward), but the adopted resolution was very strongly worded concerning the deficiencies of central management, implementation, and control and declared the responsibility of the party executive organs and the government. The text of the resolution reads:

> The Central Committee ascertained that the speeding up of economic growth did not come about in 1985–1986 and that the results of the first year of the seventh five-year plan are unsatisfactory. . . . The country consumed more than it produced. . . . Macroeconomic planning, central management, and the institutional system did not contribute to the needed extent to the improvement of inside and outside equilibrium and to finding new resources for speeding up the economy. We did not succeed in harmonizing national and firm-level interests. . . . The development of the system of macroeconomic management was inconsistent. The responsibility for the deficiencies of direction, execution, and control lies with the executive organs of the Central Committee and the government.[72]

This harsh criticism was followed by personnel changes. At the end of 1986 two knowledgeable economic members of the government were discharged with a pension: the minister of finance and the chairman of the Planning Office, the latter a deputy prime minister. Both had had long careers in the Ministry of Finance and the Planning Office before being promoted to their ministerial posts. The economic guild held them to be competent people who were the least to blame for errors and for the country going astray. In June 1987, Ferenc Havasi, the secretary for economic affairs of the Central Committee and member of the Political Committee, who had obtained the former post in 1978 and had "mastered the trade" during hard years of learning, was also demoted. At the same time György Lázár, who had held the post of prime minister for twelve years, was replaced by Károly Grósz who also became the party's general secretary in May 1988. Lázár, an undeniably failed and discredited ex–prime minister, was given the post of party deputy general secretary, and Havasi was replaced by Miklós Németh. In early summer 1987, other personnel changes in the leading apparatus of the party were carried out (new, younger faces appeared) without impairing the authority of the Kádár leadership.

This first series of events ended when the Central Committee of the Hungarian Socialist Workers' party adopted a political resolution that was intended to outline "the social-economic program of deployment" in early July 1987[73] and the new prime minister presented Parliament with a Stabilization Working Program based on that resolution in September.[74] As the first steps of its realization, a draft bill on the value added tax and another on the personal income tax were submitted, but the new government program—although progressive in its conception—lacked any detail other than those measures.

The second series of events began with a study dealing mainly with the economy. A few researchers in a small research institute of the Ministry of Finance tried to sum up their views on the state of the Hungarian economy, on the chances of its recovery, and on recommendations in a study entitled "Turnover and Reform." There were of course many antecedents on which the authors could rely, previous publications and debates that analyzed certain causes of the present situation, diagnosed it from individual standpoints, and discussed the chances of recovery. The study outlined the negligence, hesitation, and wrong decisions of the leadership. As for the tasks of the future, the document urged a comprehensive and conceptual reorganization of the economy and the political system, a recommendation that was on the whole accepted—even if some details were challenged—by the majority of knowledgeable people. The study, which was rewritten several times, was widely debated during the first months of 1987 in different forums of the Patriotic People's Front, in youth clubs and camps, by university and firm-level debating societies, and on television and radio programs. Its text was broadcast by the Hungarian transmission of Radio Free Europe.

The party leaders were ambivalent toward the wide-scale debate surrounding "Turnover and Reform." On one hand they could not but accept on the whole the critique and the positive program that the study contained. On the other hand the party leadership believed that the critical part of the study was one-sided and exaggerated. Of the propositions, the ideas (or a large part of them) concerning changes in property relations, the easing of the country's Comecon orientation, and the necessity of political reform were unacceptable. What irritated official circles most was the wide publicity the text received, and party disciplinary action was initiated against some of the party-member authors and specialists who actively supported the study and organized debates, on the grounds that they were promoting ideas that did not conform to party resolutions.

The most important turn of events concerning "Turnover and Reform" occurred in April 1987. After many accusations of being suspect and oppositionist, the study was discussed in an Economic Workshop of the

Central Committee, which included renowned scientists, firm managers, and government and party officials and was led by the party's secretary for economy. Not long after the workshop, a shortened version of the study was published by the economic journal of the Hungarian Academy of Sciences together with some conceptual and detailed comments. In the same issue of the journal, the standpoint of the workshop concerning "Turnover and Reform," agreeing with it on the whole, was also published.[75]

The two series of events that started in the fall of 1986 crossed one another in May and June of 1987, and there were many common aspects of the study discussed in the Economic Workshop, the party resolution of July 1987, and both the critical and the conceptual parts of the government program presented in September. This correlation was partly owing to the fact that some of the authors of "Turnover and Reform" took part in the preparation of the official documents.

Let me enumerate only the main tasks figuring in both the study and the two official documents: to reestablish economic equilibrium and in doing so, to halt the growth of debt in convertible currencies, even if that task necessitated the reduction of personal consumption (and real wages); to adapt the structure of the economy to world market needs and requirements; to create a true market economy with the tools of its operation; to achieve deregulation and a tax system that did not differentiate among the different forms of ownership (this point could not be left out of the documents, if only because the relevant draft bills were already in a very advanced state); to monetarize the economy; to create possibilities for circulation of capital; to devalue the forint and thereby do away with individual export incentives and import restrictions; to create preconditions that would attract direct foreign investment; and to initiate changes in planning, the functions of the plan, and the political system needed if the country were to adapt to the exigencies of a market economy. The text of "Turnover and Reform" was naturally much more outspoken in treating those problems than the party and government documents. For example, the study (shortened version) starts its treatment of the problems of the next phase of the reform with the following:

> The main question is whether we can create a true socialist market economy in the competitive sector and planning based on the comprehensive regulating role of the market. We need a social environment that rewards entrepreneurship, that is oriented toward business success and not toward avoiding failure, that is able to manage conflicts arising in a market process.[76]

Compared to this wording, the July party document is very cautious: "An active role is to be accorded to commodity and money relations;

to supply and demand; to credit, prices, exchange rates, efficiency, and profitability."[77] The text of the September government program is much more resolute and progressive: "One of the main tools of implementing the program is to expand competition and market mechanisms and to create the preconditions of a less constrained movement of capital."[78]

Károly Grósz's debut in Parliament as prime minister was decidedly successful. It was quite normal for the government program and the tax bills to be adopted by an overwhelming majority (before summer 1988 Parliament accepted every bill and resolution unanimously), but in his speech, comments, and press conference—all transmitted by live television and later in an edited version—he came across as a knowledgeable, argumentative, determined, and dynamic politician. As a contrast, the government program was recommended to Parliament in the name of the party by János Kádár who made a bad impression. He was long, hesitating, and repeated old catchphrases.

The remaining months of 1987 passed under the spell of preparations for 1988. The apparatus was busy working on the preparations of the new tax laws coming into force on 1 January 1988 and the related price changes, and it was decided to give all Hungarian citizens a new passport. With this passport and minimum of $60 in their pockets (and a bank certificate showing its legal source), they could travel abroad essentially unconstrained.[79] Still, the changeover was not a smooth one. There were reorganizations among the ministries and government committees. Ministers were dismissed, and along with the organizational changes, some old members of the government obtained new posts.

In the meantime, the ordinary people also prepared for 1988. As a result of the preannounced 15 percent price rise, a record retail trade turnover was registered in the last months of 1987. Money was drawn from personal savings accounts to make purchases, and following the buy-up wave there were serious shortages, first in construction materials and later in several durable consumer goods.

The first months of 1988 were months of calculation for the population. People looked at the new, higher prices and checked whether or not the wage accounting department had made an error in calculating their new wages (gross with personal income tax). The general rule was to raise gross wages to the extent that given the new, higher personal income taxes, they remained at their old level. In the light of the new, progressive income tax, people weighed the desirability of overtime or second jobs and the possibilities of earning extra income and concealing it from the tax authorities. They pondered how to set up the family budget under the harsher conditions. Long queues before the passport windows indicated a strong desire to travel, and the most practical people went to Vienna to buy goods that could be sold at home with a markup.

The people experienced a marked deterioration in their standard of living, and public malaise was increased by the fact that many large firms, being in financial crisis, had to reduce their work forces. The jobs of many thousands of people were discontinued in large metallurgic areas (first of all in northeastern Hungary) without their being offered any other employment.

The leadership was the cause of further disillusionment in the country. Party and nonparty, politically involved and uninvolved people all had hoped that the tax and price "reforms"—bitter pills for everybody—would be followed by steps that would radically change the totality of economic-social relations. But the fact that there was no headway in this regard—thinly veiled by small and unimportant measures—prevailed.

Party members were also concerned about intraparty events. During the first months of 1988, individual conversations were held with every member as part of the process of issuing new membership cards. As a result of these conversations, some 45,000 party members (5–6 percent of the total) declared that they did not wish to renew their membership. Also, two new documents were presented for intraparty debate, one dealing with the role of the party and the other with ideological problems, but the membership felt that neither document gave acceptable answers to present problems. There was a genuine disillusionment on the part of the membership and a distrust of the leadership. People spoke of the conservatism of the Kádárian center and urged its demotion and/or replacement.

All of these events in domestic politics led to the breakthrough discussed at the beginning of this chapter: to the radical changes in the composition of the leading party bodies and to the gaining of ground of the reform wing.

With regard to world politics, the country's external environment also urged that the Hungarian people prepare to reenter the stage. This outlook was the result of the gradual spreading of Gorbachev's policy, the first steps in the Soviet Union in the direction of reform, treaties and agreements between the Soviet Union and the United States, mutual concessions in crises spots all over the world, and the beginning of the Soviet Union's withdrawal from Afghanistan. One incentive for continuing the new Hungarian reform offensive was its positive acceptance in developed capitalist countries. This effect was demonstrated not only by Hungary's ability to draw ever new credit, despite the country's precarious foreign debt position. It was demonstrated also by the fact that Grósz, during his short, one-and-a-half-year term as prime minister, visited nine capitalist countries (among them the Federal Republic of Germany, Great Britain, the United States, Spain, and France) and had official discussions with heads of government, leading politicians, and business people.

In Hungary in late 1988, there was open organization, spreading, and demonstrating by alternative movements, parties in *statu nascendi*—a peculiar phenomenon for a socialist country. A dialogue was started between them and the ruling party and government in order to reach a mutually acceptable compromise. The Hungarian Socialist Workers' party itself was in the process of transforming into a party of internal debate, in which different opinions clash openly and whose leaders represent often different—even if not totally different—opinions. Political organizations close to the party or functioning in the past under party direction, such as the Communist Youth Organization or "official" trade unions, were adopting more and more independent platforms and increasingly playing the role of pressure groups emancipated from party and government tutelage. This process was also being propelled by the formation of new youth organizations and trade unions outside the TUC. As a part of a true political reform the party was preparing laws guaranteeing basic human rights and establishing the frameworks of a legal state and a new constitution, and it was hoped that these measures would constitute the framework of a future multiparty system in Hungary.

I close this discussion of the political processes in 1987 and 1988 with an excerpt from a speech delivered to the November session of Parliament by Imre Pozsgay, minister without portfolio.

> Granting that the economy has a crucial part in a country's life, I surmise that the reform is not primarily economic in its nature for the causes of economic problems and antagonisms also lie in the social sphere. Departing from this statement, the first task of the reform is to take the necessary steps in order to humanize the political system. Even if the order was not such during history, now we have first to discard obstacles in politics in order to secure the economic bases of national well-being, for Stalinist state socialism, the prime mover of central will, was also installed in the first instance politically, i.e., from above.[80]

Economic Processes

As for the macroeconomic processes of 1987 and 1988, there was a slow movement toward equilibrium and a reduction of domestic consumption. During those two years GDP produced grew (in constant prices) by 6 percent, taking into account the small improvement in the terms of trade, and domestic consumption grew at the same time by only 3 percent. Consumption falling behind production results in a slowing down of the process of indebtedness. In 1986 the deficit of the country's trade account in convertible currencies was $540 million, and that of the current account (interest payments included) was $1.4 billion.

In 1987 the trade account was almost in equilibrium, but the deficit of the current account reached $850 billion. In 1988, despite a trade-account surplus of several hundred million dollars, there was a current-account deficit of $500 million, and the $1.1-billion interest payment in 1988 constituted 4–5 percent of GDP produced. The chairman of the Hungarian National Bank publicly confessed in the fall of 1988 that of Hungary's dollar claim abroad, $3.3 billion was "interest-free." If we deduct this amount from accounts receivable, we arrive at a figure for the net interest-paying debt of $13.4 billion, which was 60 percent of GDP.[81]

The source of rising domestic consumption is accumulation and within that, investment. The volume of investment in both 1987 and 1988 surpassed the level of 1986 by 7 percent. Real wages decreased in those two years in conformity with government intentions—and the decision was unavoidable indeed—by 10–11 percent, which means that real wages in 1988 were at their level of fifteen years before. Compared to the peak level of ten years earlier, i.e., 1978, real wages in 1988 were 15–16 percent less. Consumer prices rose during these two years by 26 percent, with an attendant nominal wage rise of 14 percent. The bulk of the real wage reduction fell in 1988. On 1 January 1988, a new system of turnover tax was introduced as part of the comprehensive tax reform, and as a result, consumer prices rose in 1988 by 16 percent. At the same time, under the system of strict state-level wage regulation, wages could not rise more than 6–7 percent. The drop in total real income of the population was not more than 4 percent, however, because transfer payments by the government (pensions, family allowances) were increased to partially compensate for the price rise.

Total consumption of the population grew in 1987 compared to 1986 by 3 percent, but it fell in 1988 by the same amount. The difference between these data and the figures for real wages and real income of the population may be explained by the using up of reserves. In 1987 interest-bearing private accounts decreased by 7 billion forints whereas in previous years they had increased yearly by 10–15 billion forints.

In order to reduce the deficit on the current account, the government envisaged further restrictions in 1989. According to projections, total consumption of the population would fall by 1 percent, real income by 2–3 percent, and consumer prices would rise by 12–14 percent, nominal wages by 7–8 percent. One can expect that finding a job would be more difficult for unskilled workers.

During a period of stagnation—decrease of private consumption, strong decrease of real wages, rise in unemployment—there are uneven effects on different strata of the population. The well-to-do, the people with a flat, car, well-equipped household, and a good job, are affected the least. Much more is felt by the people living on a small pension, those having a large family, workers in large cities who cannot find a second job, the population of those areas (especially northeastern) in which industrial employment is dependent on smokestack industries (coal mining, metallurgy), and a large part of the young generation, who cannot obtain from their parents the material assistance necessary for starting an independent life. These strata have serious problems during years of stagnation and fallback, and in Hungary, there is not much chance that they can improve their lot in the coming years. It is understandable that their desperation increases, which plays a role in the perceptible rise in criminal activities (causing widespread fear). It is also understandable that because of low and deteriorating wages in Hungary, educated young intellectuals and workers with skills that are most in demand increasingly try to work abroad, especially in the developed capitalist countries.

Tensions between justified (or allegedly justified) social needs and the possibilities of the state budget have intensified. This fact was most clearly demonstrated during discussions in parliamentary committees on the 1989 budget, which were amply reported in the press and on television and radio (something never done before). Deputies in the various committees said that the budget proposal was insufficient for the maintenance of existing health and educational institutions and also for remedying social problems caused by inflation (especially in the case of those people who have small pensions or large families). It was also pointed out that young people were not able to become independent for want of government assistance in buying flats of their own. As a result of these debates, and some sporadic street demonstrations, the government had to give in and reduce real expenses of the central administration and defense by 10 percent.

An Economic Policy to Establish a Market Economy

The Tax Reform

On 1 January 1988 the new laws on the general turnover tax and the personal income tax came into force, and on 1 January 1989 the law on entrepreneurial profit tax, adopted during the fall 1988 session of Parliament, also became valid. The introduction of the new *turnover tax* (called the General Turnover Tax, GTT) ensured the lucidity of the whole tax system because it restricted the possibilities of using different methods to tax enterprises, and businesses. At the same time, a whole range of different kinds of taxes formerly levied on firms (the so-called wage tax, accumulation tax, regional development tax, etc.) was eliminated.

The rates of the general turnover tax are 0, 15, and 25 percent. There is no tax on fuel, food, or personal transport (instead, these items are heavily subsidized). Other services are taxed at 15 percent, and all the remaining consumer prices include a 25 percent turnover tax. The new turnover tax was introduced following the Western European practice as a value added tax.[82] Technically, the 15 percent price rise envisaged by the government for 1988 had to result from the introduction of this tax.

The *personal income tax* is levied on the total (aggregate) yearly income of every individual (not family). This principle is a sound one compared to the previous practice of taxing different sources of income separately. Attached to this new tax is a pension contribution of 10 percent on wages and salaries. The tax table is progressive even at the low end. It starts with 20 percent for incomes well under the average wage (with the pension contribution, the levy is 30 percent) and reaches the maximum 60 percent in the 600,000-forint-and-over income bracket. The tax rate for a skilled worker with an average wage is 39 percent (i.e., 49 percent with the pension contribution) so that any income above this level is taxed at a rate of at least 50 percent.

Two strata are partially exempt from the general system of personal income taxation: agricultural smallholders and intellectuals. The government feared that a tough tax system would have negative repercussions on market-oriented small-scale agricultural production and that producers would reduce their activity to self-sufficiency, which would endanger the supply of agricultural products. According to the tax rules, therefore, gross income from agricultural small production under 500,000 forints (i.e., for the majority of smallholders) is tax free. For intellectuals, the rule is that copyright fees, royalties, the pay for guest professors, etc., are included in the tax base at a reduced rate: Only 35 percent of such income is taxed. This measure was motivated in several ways, but the crux of the matter is that the government did not want to infuriate intellectuals.

The new rules outlining the general turnover tax and the personal income tax were prepared in a comparatively short time. (For similar changes in the tax system, generally three to four years are needed in order to have enough time for debate by specialists, society at large, and Parliament.) The proposals were enacted into law during the September 1987 session of Parliament and they came into force on 1 January 1988. Because of the shortage of time, debate was restricted and formal, but there are justified criticisms of the proposals and the laws.[83]

The new taxes conform in their structure with the requirements of the reform, but their speedy introduction, and the fact that they were not coordinated with other reform steps, cannot be accepted either from a specialist or from a social-policy point of view. It was wrong and politically harmful to introduce the new turnover tax when there was a general increase in the price of consumer goods, because the people then realize unavoidable and heavy real wage reduction as the consequence of "reform steps." Of the two possibilities of a one-phase turnover tax and the officially backed value added tax, the former would have been a better choice. The latter causes considerable surplus work for firm-level administrations, which makes the alleged advantages of the value added tax negligible.

In the system of personal income taxation, the tax rates are exaggerated and draw away a very high portion of what are already low personal incomes. The negative effects are twofold. People will increasingly try to conceal their income or channel it into forms that are easier to disguise, and former experience shows that tax authorities are helpless in the face of mass tax fraud. Even more important is the fact that since the tax reduces the incentive to earn, people will work less instead of more. Both of these effects materialized during 1988, and the government intended to reduce rates and the progressivism of the personal income tax in 1989.

The third element of the new tax system conforms with the exigencies of a market economy, and it was the rate of the *entrepreneurial profit tax* that was largely debated. The government argued that profit drawn away from firms was 74 percent in 1987, and 60 pecent in 1988 so that the 55 percent rate planned for 1989 was in fact a reduction. In the end, Parliament adopted a 50 percent tax, which firm managers still consider to be too high. The financial government agencies declared, however, that with only a 50 percent entrepreneurial tax, the budget deficit could not be held within reasonable limits.[84]

The three above-mentioned tax laws are generally valid laws, unlike previously when implementation was riddled with exceptions. If one disregards the excessive severity of the personal income tax, it conforms with the needs of a market economy and makes it impossible for the government to use the tax system to manipulate the position of individual firms through a host of decrees and ordinances. At the same time—and this fact should be stressed—the tax laws refer to state firms, cooperatives, *and* private ventures and the personal incomes derived from them. Formerly taxes were differentiated according to ownership, the use to which the income was put (wages or investment), and the types of personal income— not to mention the many exemptions. The new taxes reflect implicitly the new thinking on ownership in that they conform with the requirements of a competitive mixed economy and lay the foundation—from a tax point of view—for changes in ownership relations.

Preparations for Changes in Ownership Relations

A company law adopted in October 1988 concerns ownership relations explicitly and replaces many previously uncoordinated and fragmented regulations. The law was drawn up after many specialist debates and is a mature, detailed piece of legislation, one that makes an able use of foreign experiences.

The company law places the most popular organizational forms of business activity in market economies—i.e., the limited joint-stock company, the syndicate, the limited-liability company, the joint-stock company, the unlimited company, etc.—into a well-defined, unitary, coordinated legal framework. The law also regulates the internal relations of the various partnerships. For example, for joint-stock companies it defines how to form and operate the general assembly, the board of directors, and the supervisory committee and outlines their mutual relations.

The company law makes it possible for private capital and private persons to participate in joint-stock companies and to sell and buy stocks issued by joint-stock companies that have a nonprivate majority. Private capital is constrained by the law—purely private companies cannot employ more than 500 people—and it is not likely that there will be any demand in the foreseeable future to form private ventures of such dimensions. The law also defines the conditions of foreign capital participation. There are no restrictions on foreign capital participation in any Hungarian company (including the private ones) up to a 50 percent share, but total or preponderantly foreign partnerships need the permission of the minister of finance and the minister of trade (permission is to be considered granted if it is not denied in ninety days).

The company law is based on the notion of a mixed economy and cooperation among the different forms of ownership. It lays the foundations of a capital market, capital flows among entrepreneurs, and the participation of foreign capital in Hungarian business activity. It creates the legal basis for the utilization of the accumulated money wealth of the population as capital by legalizing the capitalization of income, the income from capital, and the right to receive dividends.

In anticipation of the law's coming into effect on 1 January 1989, there was a kind of decentralization among state firms in 1988. Some large multiplant firms gave autonomy to their plants (factories) by organizing them as joint-stock companies. The plants owned one another's stocks, and the firms' headquarters were transformed into holding centers. In other instances, bank credits were converted into stock in a new company. Company leaderships (company councils and other leading bodies) were forced to take this step because of pressure from the creditor banks. Some firms chose the joint-stock-company-cum-holding-center form in order to uphold their integrity in the face of some future government decentralization campaign. There were some plants that decidedly stepped out of the large company framework, an action generally initiated by adventurous local leaders who hoped to thus improve the performance and sphere of action of the said unit.

All of those events were marginal however. The company law regulates the foundation of new partnerships, *not* the transformation of existing firms into the partnership form. There has to be an answer, however, to the question of what to do with the huge block of state enterprises and cooperatives (cooperatives in name only) that constitute—the many recent innovations notwithstanding—the dominant sector of the Hungarian economy.

Firms belonging to this sector do not conform to the exigencies of a market economy. They are overweight, have many plants, and enjoy an artificial monopoly position. In addition, their new management forms introduced in the middle of the 1980s (company councils, etc.) are not satisfactory from the point of view of the ownership because they do not solve the problem of market-based capital allocation. In small and medium-sized units, for which only a little capital is required and in which workers can grasp the whole of the production and sales activities, the drive for perpetuating the company, and with it the workplace, may result in a satisfactory functioning and a growth of capital. In large firms however, employing several thousand people and concentrating huge amounts of capital, things are different. The prime goal in these firms is for workers to earn more, and worker representatives sitting on company councils cannot neglect this interest if they want to be true representatives of the workers. On the other hand, managers operating and developing their own firms have too local an orientation to be able to utilize social capital well.

In order to create a market economy, therefore, it is necessary to transform large state firms and large cooperatives into some form of partnership regulated by the company law (and to decentralize them somewhat in the process). The government intends to regulate this transition process by a so-called transition act. There are fierce debates among specialists concerning this act, and I can sketch only the conceptual problems and the main differing points of view. I have to add at the same time that many of the details behind these concepts were not worked out in time to meet the deadline of the first half of 1989.

Specialists agree that in the case of smaller state firms or smaller units that leave the larger firm the present forms of self-government should be retained and that the company council, the general assembly, or the assembly of delegates should retain all property rights. Other firms however should be transformed into joint-stock companies, and this is where the debate starts. Who will be the stockholders and how should the conversion be managed?

The majority of the specialists reject the possibility that a state firm should acquire the majority of its own shares and become its own proprietor. Many people are of the opinion that shares of would-be joint-stock companies should be given to newly formed state capital-holding centers, which would buy and sell shares and other securities to and from other participants on the economic scene. Other people think that the main shareholders should be the state-owned business banks and unit trusts depending from them, by converting part of the outstanding long-term credits into shares. One popular idea is to give the shares of state firms to insurance companies, pension funds, and institutions whose expenses are financed from the budget (e.g., universities, health centers, and local councils) and reduce the budgetary provision of those institutions by a conservative estimate of their dividend income. This solution is sensible in that it gives into the hands of well-defined strata of the population control over how wisely their deputies act in security transactions.[85]

The three solutions are not divided from one another by impenetrable difficulties, nor do they exclude one another. The participants of the debates themselves ponder on how to combine them. In the crux of the matter, i.e., that a market economy in Hungary undeniably needs the transformation of state firms into companies and the operation of a securities market, with various types of owners there is total agreement.

The debate is on how to manage the transformation. Some people believe that it should be an act of the government. Others prefer that the company council (or the general assembly or the assembly of delegates) decide whether a firm should become a joint-stock company or not. With the declaration of a changeover, the property rights of the company council cease, and its role is reduced to that of a mere participative organ. The changeover may be in the interest of the firm itself, as by issuing shares it could raise new capital. At the same time, central management can encourage the transformation, and it could be a precondition in the case of government subsidies, government investment contribution, or government-assisted financial reorganization.

The second solution has the advantage that it implies a natural process of transformation. Some people fear, however, that company councils will not be willing to part with their prerogatives or that firm managers will perhaps think that control over them might be stricter under the new system than the control imposed by the company councils. Such considerations argue in favor of realizing the change through government action. Part of the changes should be combined with decentralization, some of which might be initiated by joint-stock-companies themselves, especially in the case of firms heading toward bankruptcy. On the other hand, capital owners may be interested in preserving large company frameworks and monopoly positions, so it has been suggested that antitrust legislation and attached institutions should be introduced.

The transformation of large agricultural cooperatives operating many thousands of hectares that have totally lost their cooperative character should be promoted by modifying the rights of such cooperatives. The process would be facilitated if the members were given the right to decide by secret ballot about the decentralization and splitting up of existing cooperatives. Modernization would be enhanced by a radical extension of the rental system within cooperatives, also to be decided by secret ballot. Secret ballots are important because both of these solutions impair the power of the present leaders. As a more complicated but more radical solution, one could think of transforming the cooperatives into companies. In this way, the wealth of a cooperative would be divided among the members, who would obtain shares that incorporated property rights (perhaps with restricted transferability). Such changes could be precipitated by the reduction of subsidies given to cooperatives and deteriorating income positions, which would urge leaders and members to take a bold step. At the same time, an incentive could be given to the changeover by making reorganization a requirement in order to receive credits from the commercial banks and the state budget.[86]

There are some privatization ideas, too. There is no question that private capital could become the dominant proprietor in state firms by buying up the shares, because there is not enough purchasing power in the hands of the population to do so. But instead of retaining and scaling up the rental system in the retail and catering spheres, there are plans to hand over such state property to those private entrepreneurs who offer the most for it. There is also a faint idea of solving the problems of weak, bankrupt agricultural cooperatives by privatizing them.

Deregulation, Liberalization

The measures cited thus far constitute only a part of the preconditions of unfolding market forces. In the second half of 1988, the government began professional, committee-based work with the participation of well-known specialists to elaborate a detailed, matter-of-fact program to bring about a market economy in Hungary, and it is interesting that this work was organized by the same Rezsö Nyers who was the leading personality during the reform preparations of 1966–1968. Even in the steps planned for 1989 the government followed the theses of this reform conception, and further elaboration was to come later.[87] In addition to what has been done so far, the institutions and personnel necessary to carry out a monetary policy, and within that a money-and-securities market, have to be developed.[88] In 1989, the government intended to start further deregulation and liberalization processes.

The unified tax system is a deregulatory act in itself, as is the right given to Parliament to set up limits for state subsidies that the government cannot transgress without special authorization. Deregulation has been aided by the fact that as a result of hard bargaining in parliamentary committees, the government had to cut administrative and defense expenses in the 1989 budget by 10 percent.

Liberalization is likely in wages of the state and cooperative sectors, in prices, and in convertible-currency imports. Separate wage regulation was to be abolished by 1989, and wage-level and wage relations were then to be influenced by a system of institutionalized bargaining. The market will have a greater impact on prices as the range of free (market-based) prices grows, and there will be fewer administrative price prescriptions. As a result of import liberalization, import competition and the impact of foreign-trade prices will be reinforced. According to advance information in product groups representing 40 percent of the convertible-currency trade, especially machinery and parts embodying new technologies and certain consumer goods, firms will be able to import freely. Such a partial liberalization of imports necessitates a sizable devaluation of the forint, which will boost exports and reduce export subsidies (which has deregulative effects in itself). All of this planning is a step toward convertibility of the forint, a goal for the distant future. In a small country such as Hungary, the market and within it the capital market cannot function properly without a convertible (or at least partially convertible) currency.

It should be kept in mind that the planned deregulative and liberalization steps will be carried out in an economically vulnerable, highly indebted country. The desirable, nay indispensable, structural changes must be brought about under minimal or even zero growth conditions, and this fact requires a highly restrictive monetary policy. Under such circumstances even desirable changes endanger individual positions and may also raise unemployment. Therefore, it is particularly hard to calibrate the deregulation and liberalization steps properly. One has to maneuver between Scylla and Charybdis: If the steps are too small, they will be ineffective and do more harm than good; if they are too bold, they may cause shock, generate inadmissible inflation, and thereby lead the country into a state of revolt and anarchy. Only the future will prove whether Hungary has found the path leading toward a functioning market economy built around mixed ownership.

Summary

The developments and processes in Hungary during 1987 and 1988 may be characterized by three interdependent tendencies. First, the political-social climate in Hungary was hectic and unstable. There was widespread uncertainty concerning material conditions because the standard of living stagnated or deteriorated, which had an effect on the public mood and conditions in general. Criminality was on the rise. Alternative, independent pressure groups and political organizations appeared on the scene, and in the ruling party itself—or more exactly, the party in whose name autocratic power is exerted at the top and medium levels—important changes were felt. The forces of democratization came to the fore, and it was believed that the solution lay in a pluralistic political structure.

Second, the shape of the Hungarian economy deteriorated rather than improved. In 1988 real wages dropped drastically, personal consumption moderately, and this tendency was likely to continue into 1989. At the same time, the inequalities in living conditions and life opportunities grew. Lack of money impeded the functioning of education, health services, and scientific institutions. Furthermore, it was becoming more and more difficult for young people to establish their own household (e.g., to obtain a flat and to buy durable goods). The piling up of debt and debt-servicing liabilities slowed down but did not stop. All of these factors constrained economic policy to within narrow limits.

Third, the establishment of the institutions of a market economy speeded up, and with negligible exceptions, the business activity of private and foreign capital was set free. The government intended to soon make further important changes toward a market economy with respect to the operation of state firms. As a result the growth of capital would be the central goal of state firms too, and market mechanisms of capital allocation would deploy. One has to surmise, however, that the effect of these changes in the expectations and endeavors of the market participants will be felt only after a lag of some years.

8

Summary and Outlook·

Instead of writing a comprehensive history or trying to build a model of the Hungarian economy, I have tried to write an account of events in Hungary for those people who too are unfamiliar with that or indeed any socialist system. I believe that the reform of 1968, which moved Hungary (however haltingly) toward a socialist market economy, was an important departure from the "classical" socialist economy that originated in the Soviet Union. It is worth noting that the very successful changes adopted in China in the 1980s were in many ways based on the Hungarian experience; likewise, Gorbachev's *perestroika* and the subsequent economic renewal in several Eastern European countries have numerous points in common with events that began in Hungary some twenty years ago. The mistakes and the fact that Hungary's reform was halted at one stage may also prove instructive.

Hungary's reform began while there was still time for it to work. It would have been better had market forces been introduced into the economy earlier, during the post-1956 consolidation perhaps, but even in 1968 the changes were not made in an atmosphere of crisis. The leadership acted pragmatically in the face of a minor recession and pessimistic forecasts. Old dogmas, if not rejected outright, were cautiously pushed aside. The reform suffered from problems, including conscious and unconscious compromises, but these were growing pains. Conflicts did arise—in part because of the natural outgrowths of a market economy, in part because of compromises and mistakes—for example, there was tension between company autonomy and the old ministerial system of economic management, and there was the lack of a capital market. The leadership did not take charge and solve these problems by moving further toward the market, though there were proposals in this direction. Instead, following old habits, the government waved the banners of planning and the "public interest" and turned matters over to the bureaucracy and the party apparatus. Thus the bureaucracy's power over the economy, established in the 1950s and shaken in 1968, was reinforced even though economic management was now indirect.

There were international forces, both economic and political, that helped derail the reform, but the most important obstacles were internal. This fact was acknowledged by Károly Grósz during his first visit as prime minister to Moscow in 1987. In a toast, Grósz made the following statement, unprecedented for a top Hungarian official:

> Although we suffered serious losses in our foreign markets, we are well aware that our problems are largely domestic. We realized the need for change several decades ago. Our reform policy and all our actions are a testimony to this. . . . Based on this experience, we can confidently say that our greatest error was not being persistent enough—partly because of pressure from the international environment—in carrying out our reform policy.[89]

The system of indirect management, together with the mistaken notion that Hungary could accelerate its growth through Comecon trade, rendered the country unable to cope with a world economic restructuring that was itself misdiagnosed as temporary. Rigidities inherited from the 1960s caused a decline in the terms of trade, and the country compensated for this decline with hard-currency loans obtained on favorable terms. But the loans were not spent to modernize the economy. In part, they went to maintain consumption at its previous rate; in part, they funded centrally mandated, raw material- and energy-intensive investments, thus perpetuating Hungary's obsolete economic structure. Recession was therefore a necessity. In 1978 only 90 percent of domestic consumption covered by GDP was realized, and the hard-currency debt rose to 150 percent of yearly hard-currency exports.

The crisis finally spurred the leadership to action, but the danger of default remained. A twofold therapy was indicated. On the one hand, dramatic steps were needed to meet the crisis: reducing domestic consumption, raising hard-currency exports, and restricting imports. On the other hand, these steps would only address symptoms; the deeper malaise also had to be fought.

The attack on the symptoms was a success, to the extent that any such program can be truly successful. Hungary avoided a default, and its debt declined for a few years. This result had a lot to do with the leadership's resolve, but the indirect system of management played an even greater role. As a way of controlling individual companies' activities, this management system lent itself readily to the tasks at hand. One might say that the system and the bureaucracy running it had found a task worthy of them.

The deeper therapy was not a success. The government acknowledged that the economic system was at the heart of the problem and that the answer lay in a return to the original reform objective, the establishment of a true socialist market economy. The government added that the reform program would have to be modified in light of experience to include a selective investment policy that favored efficient exporting for hard currency.

These were sound ideas, but acting on them was another story. Progressive and theoretically important changes proved marginally effective at best. They could not tease successful innovation out of businesses when investment funds were being cut in order to limit domestic consumption and weak firms were being subsidized at the expense of strong ones. The debt crisis continued (with minor fluctuations in severity), and indirect economic management grew increasingly harsh and discriminatory. Firm-level initiative, the only way out of the debt crisis, was further suppressed. The economy was beset by a vicious circle of mutually reinforcing recessionary pressures, stagnation, and mounting debt.

The events of the last ten or fifteen years can be interpreted as having been determined by geopolitics.[90] It can be argued that Hungary is a small country, poor in natural resources, and on the periphery of—and fifteen to twenty years behind—the mainstream of development. Its membership in Comecon and the Warsaw Pact (so the argument goes) prevents it from joining in Western Europe's economic integration. These factors assign Hungary a place among the moderately developed, heavily indebted countries. Most of these countries underwent intense industrialization in the late 1960s and early 1970s, creating or enlarging capacity in traditional manufacturing industries. They took on massive foreign debts during the credit boom of the 1970s in order to finance this industrialization and the infrastructure it required. At the same time, the advanced industrial countries were entering the so-called third industrial revolution.

The technology and development gaps grew as the new industries in the moderately developed nations proved to be rather uncompetitive. Those nations responded by trying to modernize their economies and export more efficiently. Experience shows that such modernization works best in countries where multinationals are present, through either direct investment or subsidiaries, and as a socialist country Hungary is not a particularly inviting place for multinationals. Still, among the heavily indebted countries, Hungary is in fairly good shape. It did not default. It has a reasonably good credit rating in the major capital markets even though, in the second half of the 1980s, its net hard-currency debt was more than twice its annual hard-currency exports. Hungary's efforts are appreciated in banking circles.

These factors are real, but they do not fully explain the situation. Hungary could have stuck with its reform program in the early 1970s, and later in that decade it could have embarked on even bolder, better-coordinated reforms. The debt crisis could have been handled as part of the comprehensive reform process, or at least in a way that did not discard the reform. Such a course would have produced conflict but would also have created a more modern, flexible, and competitive economy, one that would have been easier to integrate into the international division of labor. If Hungary had done these things, it might have emerged by now from the most painful period of its structural adjustment; instead, it did not even begin such an adjustment.

The question is not why socialist Hungary could not overcome its historical backwardness (although Hungarians do not pose it this way). The question is why Hungary's relative position fell so far in the past decade compared to nations that were historically at a similar level, such as Spain, or at a more-developed level, such as Finland and Austria. Why did the leadership, after coming to the right conclusions and moving in the right direction, turn back? Why, so many years after the 1978 shock, has no thoughtful program of reform been presented to the public? Why have experts not been assembled and put to work like those who in 1966 prepared the way for change? Like many other people, I believe that the turning point of 1971–1972 and 1978–1980 could have led to serious change. The leadership must take most of the blame for the fact that in facing those crises, Hungary slid back. After the bold initiative of 1966–1968, the leadership grew hesitant and conservative.

Two factors were important in this regard. First, the reform movement had overstepped the bounds the leadership had assigned it, and by the early 1970s, it was clear that unleashing market forces would require more radical reform than the leadership was prepared to contemplate. Years earlier, in the planning for the 1968 reform, there had been some radical proposals, even though ideas closer to the "theoretical foundations" of socialism had won the day. In the second half of the 1970s, and particularly after 1978, these ideas were dusted off. They included the rehabilitation of the capital function, legalization of capital income, recognition of structural unemployment, an end to the dominance of big firms and the adoption of antitrust laws, expansion of the private sector, and legal restraints on the economic activities of the government and the party. These ideas were too much for the leadership. It was slow in responding to events and could not bring itself to radicalize the reform. Instead, if dithered.

Second, social conflict does not arise simply because different groups hold different ideas. It is a commonplace that behind the acceptance and rejection of ideas are people with real or perceived interests. In Hungary's case, the reform reduced the government and party bureaucracies' leverage over the economy and weakened the position of managers whose main talents were obeying their superiors and avoiding any sort of risk. A threat to the middle ranks, to the "apparatus," was a threat to the people at the top. As a source of information on events and public opinion, the apparatus helped shape the leadership's views, and the leadership, in turn, had to be able to shape the apparatus to the government's long-term goals and win its consent. The Hungarian leadership was able to do so in the 1960s, but later on the apparatus was more successful in pressing its position. This fact played no small part in the leadership's change of heart.

In 1987 and 1988 the Kádárian center began to vanish, and there was an attendant change of course in politics and the economy. There were undeniable signs of a turnaround in Hungary. The question was, whether those hopeful beginnings would lead to a breakthrough, whether a true socialist market economy, with pluralistic power relations, would develop in Hungary. There is no definite answer to the question as yet. The future is always shaped by a complicated network of economic and political factors, but without aiming at completeness, I want to present a few aspects of the relevant problems.

The necessity of the transition cannot be denied. Today, near the end of the twentieth century, we cannot imagine any other way to ensure true progress. This fact is realized by most of the people on the highest levels of power. With able political maneuvering, reaching a consensus with realistic political opposition, and assuming the responsibility for the unavoidable social shocks, a determined and unified leadership can lead the country out of its difficult situation.

We have to take into account that currently it is Hungary that has the best chance for a breakthrough among the Central and Eastern European socialist countries. The Hungarian people remember the shock of the clashes of 1956 and the years after 1966–1968 when Hungary was able to create a situation previously unheard of in a socialist environment: plenty of goods, larger possibilities for the utilization of the labor force, a more liberal public spirit, more room for thought, and criticism of central power. In an economic context it is very important that under the indirect system of management established after 1972—all of its constraints and drawbacks notwithstanding—a large part of Hungary's firm managers developed business contacts with capitalist countries and learned to think in terms of the world market. This experience, this knowledge—under favorable conditions—may serve as a foundation for further progress. At the same time—and I want to stress this point—during the post-1968 era of constriction and uncertainty large strata of the population learned how to use their knowledge and capabilities to venture into small investments. Under certain conditions (for example, an improvement of the tax system), better incentives and increased trust in government might occur, which would promote investment and entrepreneurship.

The Hungarian economy would collapse from one day to the other if international money markets withdrew their confidence and the country could not manage its international financial liabilities. But, as is well known, the collapse of the debtor is not in the interest of the creditor. At the same time, there is justification from a world political and world economic point of view for supporting Hungary's effort (or to put the matter more exactly, not to counteract it). Socialist countries as a whole are falling rapidly behind today's Europe and the world. Therefore, the danger of a new crisis spot arising in Eastern Europe is not to be underestimated. Hungary is the ripest country in this bloc for a successful emergence from this situation as a result of the reform started in 1966–1968, even if it was later "deformed." Success in Hungary would be a positive example for progressive forces in the other socialist countries that a socialist market economy can be developed.

The question of what is to be understood by a socialist market economy can be approached from several aspects. Somewhat superficially, one could say that Hungary and perhaps other socialist countries are trying to create capitalist commodity production without domination of capitalists. There is a lot of truth in this statement, because Hungary really has tried to create a system in which most of society's capital is allocated through a market mechanism. One could also stress historical factors—for example, that because of historical circumstances and socialist ideals, the politics and economics in Eastern Europe diverged in the second half of this century from the Western European and North American model. In this view, market-based socialism is a way of bridging the gap.

There is also an answer that stresses the partial validity of socialist thinking. It is true that too many fundamental ideas in socialism and communism have proved to be illusions, and it is also true that an economic system that uses self-regulating market mechanisms can provide greater well-being for the people than a system that hobbles or eliminates the market can. But it is possible to imagine a variation: a market economy that can operate, capital allocation included, without capitalists. Indeed, there would be fewer centripetal forces in such an economy to contradict long-term macroeconomic regulation. The goals of socialism—reducing inequalities of wealth and income, ensuring equality of opportunity—would not have to be abandoned, and in this sense, the use of the term *market-based socialism* is justified.

One has to declare firmly that the economic system envisaged by Hungarian reformers would be close to the system of either Sweden or Austria—of course on a lower level of development—and markedly different from both the "classic" (Stalinist) model of real socialism and the vision of the future (in Marx's own words, infant communism) cherished by Marx and the Marxian wing of the international labor movement. At the same time, the social sector of the economy in Hungary would be much larger than in either Sweden or Austria. This point can be made with certainty and not only because Hungary's reform programs stress the dominant role of social property. Under present, historically evolved circumstances, the privatization of government firms and institutions can be imagined only as a partial solution. Therefore, it is even more important to establish in Hungary a form of operating social (state) property that would incorporate capital allocation through the market, as in the market economies.

Will there be a multiparty system in Hungary? In a few years a multiparty system may arise, as this is the political system that is the most appropriate for a market economy in that it secures social control over central power and offers a more flexible functioning of political institutions. Actually I think the most relevant question today is whether the enlightened, reformist leadership of the one party in Hungary (or to put it more exactly, the reform wing that came to power in 1988) will be able to realize its program under the present political and social conditions.

The transition is not in the short-term interest of an influential strata of the population, many of them party members. Of the many facets of this problem let me mention only one (which is, however, very important). Leading officials of the government and party apparatus and the leaders of state firms and agricultural cooperatives have very close personal ties, and it often happens that people from the party apparatus or leading government officials are chosen to be chairmen of cooperatives and firms and vice versa. In these relationships, X is supported by Y, Y by Z, and Z by X. Such personal twists are advantageous for participants not only when remunerative or influential posts are being filled but also when favors are wanted—favors that in some cases border on corruption. A market economy with its more open atmosphere, more freedom for the press and mass media, and its alternative movements and the control they exert is a danger in itself for the people who have acquired certain positions and enjoy powerful relationships. This is the reason (in addition to adherence to old ideologies) why there is real resistance toward the announced new course among members of the party who hold local power posts.

In the ruling party and its leadership there are those people who recognize that without radical changes there can be no progress in Hungary. And there are others who are pushed by their daily interests into the antireformist camp. (They are not necessarily openly antireformist, but they refer to the country's ideological heritage, past results, and the dangers of change.) The contest between these groups is a true political contest, in which the reform wing needs to broaden its base not only within but also outside the party. Therefore, it is important how the contacts between the alternative organizations and the party's reform wing will develop and whether consensus on the platform of a radical reform among different currents within the party and between the party's reform wing and the alternative organizations will come about or not.

Notes

1. See Berend (1974), p. 11.
2. Ibid., p. 12.
3. Donáth (1977), p. 22.
4. Petö and Szakács (1985), pp. 37–38.
5. The data in this section are from Berend (1974), pp. 87–92.
6. *Pravda*, 2 July 1918 (author's translation).
7. *Pravda*, 5 February 1931 (author's translation).
8. Berend (1974), pp. 101–103.
9. Ibid., p. 106.
10. Petö and Szakács (1985), pp. 174–175.
11. Fazekas (1967), pp. 220–221.
12. Berend (1974), p. 162, and Timár (1981), pp. 82, 92, and 103.
13. Petö and Szakács (1985), pp. 310 and 314.
14. *Statisztikai Évkönyvek*.
15. Petö and Szakács (1985), p. 315.
16. *Statisztikai Évkönyvek*.
17. Szamuely (1986) gives a selection of documents of Hungarian reform thought. See also Bokor et al. (1957).
18. Donáth (1977), p. 88.
19. Petö and Szakács (1985), p. 365.
20. Ibid., pp. 512–513.
21. Calculated from Ehrlich et al. (1982); see also Ehrlich (1985).
22. Donáth (1977), p. 167.
23. Ibid., pp. 173–174.
24. Ibid., pp. 202 and 207.
25. The source of data here and elsewhere, unless otherwise specified, is the annual *Statistical Yearbooks* of the Hungarian Central Statistical Office.
26. *Külkereskedelmi statisztikai évkönyv* (1974), pp. 30–31.
27. Bauer (1981), pp. 116 and 136.
28. Donáth (1977), p. 183.
29. Berend (1974), p. 267.
30. Ibid., pp. 231 and 234.
31. Ibid., pp. 178–183.
32. Ferenc Jánossy wrote about the "quasi-developed" conditions of the Hungarian economy; see Jánossy (1969).
33. The first in-depth analysis of Comecon (also CMEA) relations was by Sándor Ausch (1969). On this excellent work the literature is undeservedly silent.

34. Kornai (1980), Eng. ed., p. 63.

35. See e.g., Marx (1972).

36. Theoretical-ideological problems of the changeover from war communism to the New Economic Policy are dealt with in Szamuely (1971).

37. See Péter (1954), (1956), and Kornai (1957).

38. Brus (1961).

39. See *Magyar Szocialista Munkáspárt határozatai és dokumentumai 1963–1966* (1963–1966), p. 307 (translation by the author).

40. Overviews of the reform are given in Nyers (1968) and Friss I. (1971).

41. See Tallós (1968).

42. See Csikós-Nagy (1966), (1969), and Hoch (1967).

43. See Vincze (1970).

44. See Szabó and Mandel (1966) and Sik (1966).

45. For the regulation and its ideology see Tiszai and Madarasi (1968).

46. See Tardos (1972).

47. See Révész (1972) and Wilcsek (1972).

48. On the first years and some ideas about the agenda see Gadó (1972), Jávorka (1973), and Nyers (1973).

49. See Berend (1988).

50. Hungarian foreign trade relations in the seventies are analyzed by Köves and Oblath (1981). For historic roots, present state, and perspectives of East-West relations from an Eastern European viewpoint see Köves (1980).

51. I have used Ágnes Ungvárszki's data and analysis; Ungvárszki (1986), pp. 87–93.

52. See Fazekas and Köllö (1985).

53. On the methods and driving forces of the process of centralization see Csanádiné (1979), Laky (1980), Laki (1982), Szalay (1982), and Köhegyi (1985).

54. On the inception of the agricultural system, its results and weaknesses, and the open problems of present agricultural policy see Gönczi (1983) and Sipos and Halmai (1988).

55. See Bauer (1975) and Nyers and Tardos (1981).

56. The analysis of the indirect management system was worked out by László Antal; Antal (1985).

57. See *Plan Econ Report*, pp. 2 and 3.

58. In this section, I have used Antal's manuscript; Antal (1987).

59. On the state of the economy and the chances of recovery see Kornai (1982), Csikós-Nagy (1983), Bácskai and Várhegyi (1983), and Nyers and Tardos (1984).

60. See *Plan Econ Report*, p. 3.

61. See Hoch (1980) and Rácz (1980).

62. See Tardos (1985).

63. On preparations, debates, and infighting see Sárközy (1986).

64. In agriculture the bidding rental system of Tibor Liska has spread. According to this system individuals and small groups rent a cooperative's machines, sheds, animals, trucks, etc. Although the results are excellent, the

system is spreading very slowly because of bureaucratic obstacles. For information on the so-called Liska model see Bársony (1981) and Bársony and Siklaky (1984).

65. On small-scale agricultural production see Tóth (1982).

66. The first serious analysis of the functioning of the so-called second economy in Hungary is Gábor and Galasi (1981).

67. Révész (1985a).

68. See Laky (1987).

69. Antal and Várhegyi (1987) analyze in detail the bureaucratic mechanism of capital allocation.

70. Adaptation problems of Hungary and other small socialist countries are dealt with in Kádár (1987).

71. The reasons why the Hungarian economy has encountered its present troubles are given in Kornai (1987), Antal (1987), Bauer (1987), Csaba (1988), and Révész (1988).

72. *Népszabadság,* 22 November 1968, p. 1.

73. See *Népszabadság,* 4 July 1987, pp. 1–2.

74. For the text adopted by Parliament, see *Népszabadság,* 19 September 1987, pp. 5–6.

75. See *Közgazdasági Szemle* 35:6 (1988). The definitive and unabbreviated text of "Turnover and Reform" is to be found along with other political, sociological, and economic studies in *Medvetánc,* no. 2 (1987). In the same number there is a study by László Lengyel, one of the authors of "Turnover and Reform," with the title "Adalćkok a Fordulat és reform történetćhez" (Contributions to the history of turnover and reform). *Medvetánc* is the social sciences periodical of the Budapest Lóránd Eötvös University and the Karl Marx University of Economics. The journal is financed by the George Soros Foundation under the auspices of the Hungarian Academy of Sciences (George Soros is a wealthy U.S. businessman of Hungarian origin).

76. See *Közgazdasági Szemle* 35:6 (1988), p. 650.

77. See *Népszabadság,* 4 July 1987, p. 1.

78. See *Népszabadság,* 19 September 1987, p. 5, pt. 3.

79. Until January 1988 a Hungarian citizen was granted an exit visa together with a certificate to exchange about $400 worth of forints (at the official exchange rate) once every three years. In addition, he or she was allowed to travel once a year if proof was provided that expenses would be paid by a foreign host.

80. See *Népszabadság,* 25 November 1988, p. 2.

81. See the speech by Ferenc Bartha, chairman of the Hungarian National Bank, at the November 1988 session of Parliament; *Népszabadság,* 26 November 1988, p. 1.

82. According to this system every firm has to add to its sales prices a turnover tax at a prescribed rate and is authorized at the same time to deduct from the taxes due the amount of turnover taxes incorporated in inputs bought by the firm. (If the turnover tax is less than the tax content of the firm's inputs, a tax return can be requested from the Tax Office.) In this system taxes levied and taxes returned cancel out one another within the economy and the burden of tax falls on end uses, especially personal consumption.

83. See Balázsy (1987), Falusné Szikra (1987), Gergely (1987), and Koltay (1987).

84. There are considerable tax exemptions in the law that was passed. The beneficiaries are small businesses; agricultural, food processing, and food trading activities; development and diffusion of high technologies; and partnerships with partially foreign ownership.

85. The topic of property, property transfer, and transition is best dealt with by Márton Tardos in two articles: Tardos (1988a) and (1988b). Besides the works of Tardos, other published materials of interest include Balázsy (1983), Bársony (1986), Nyers (1988), and Rott (1986).

86. The transition needs clarification and regulation of many details. Thus a joint-stock company cannot be formed without a firm's real capital being revalued by outside specialists (possibly a specialized capitalist firm). The transition of agricultural cooperatives is impeded by the lack of a land market: The majority of arable land is the undivided and inalienable property of cooperatives. Unless this constraint is removed, transition is impossible.

87. The first version of these theses was written by one of the authors of "Turnover and Reform," László Antal, today an adviser of the government. Given a definite form after being discussed in committees, the theses were published in the 8 December 1988 issue of *Figyelö*.

88. The first courses in the recently founded Hungarian-French banker school and the Hungarian-U.S.-Italian manager school, both in Budapest, were held in 1989.

89. *Népszabadság*, 20 July 1987, p. 3.

90. See Kopátsy (1986).

References

ANTAL, László. 1985. *Gazdaságirányítási és pénzügyi rendszerünk a reform útján* (System of management and financing in the reform process). Budapest: Közgazdasági és Jogi Könyvkiadó.

———. 1987. Restriktív gazdaságpolitika—bizonytalan, felemás reformok—kézirat (Economic policy with restrictions—dubious reform—steps). manuscript. Budapest.

ANTAL, László; BOKROS, Lajos; CSILLAG, István; LENGYEL, László; and MATOLCSY, György. 1987. Fordulat és reform. *Közgazdasági Szemle* 34(6):642–663. Published in English as Change and Reform. *Acta Oeconomica* 38:3–4 (1987): 187–213.

ANTAL, László, and VÁRHEGYI, Éva. 1987. *Tökeáramlás Magyarországon* (Capital flow in Hungary). Budapest: Közgazdasági és Jogi Könyvkiadó.

AUSCH, Sándor. 1969. *A KGST együttmüködés helyzete, mechanizmusa, távlatai.* Budapest: Akadémiai Kiadó. Published in English as *Theory and Practice of CMEA Cooperation.* Budapest: Akadémiai Kiadó, 1972.

BÁCSKAI, Tamás, and VÁRHEGYI, Éva. 1983. A magyar gazdaság monetizálása. *Gazdaság* 17(2): 16–30. Published in English as Monetization of the Hungarian Economy. *Acta Oeconomica* 31:1–2 (1983):13–22.

BALÁZSY, Sándor. 1983. Reform és tulajdon (Reform and ownership). *Közgazdasági Szemle* 30(5):600–607.

———. 1987. Az adóreformról: Bírálat és ellenjavaslat (On tax reform: Critique and counterproposal). *Közgazdasági Szemle* 34(9):1080–1092.

BÁRSONY, Jenö. 1981. Liska Tibor koncepciója: A szocialista vállalkozás. *Valóság* 24(12):22–44. Published in English as Tibor Liska's Concept: The Socialist Entrepreneurship. *Acta Oeconomica* 28:3–4 (1982):423–455.

———. 1986. A vagyonérdekeltség kialakításának problémái (Problems related to interest in enterprise property). *Közgazdasági Szemle* 33(4):435–453.

BÁRSONY, Jenö, and SIKLAKY, István. 1984. Néhány gondolat a szocialista vállalkozásról. *Közgazdasági Szemle* 31(11):1363–1371. Published in English as Some Reflection on Socialist Enterpreneurship. *Acta Oeconomica* 34:1–2 (1985):51–64.

BAUER, Tamás. 1975. A vállalatok ellentmondásos helyzete gazdasági mechanizmusunkban (The contradictory position of the firm under the economic control system in Hungary). *Közgazdasági Szemle* 22(6):725–735.

———. 1981. *Tervgazdaság, beruházás, ciklusok* (Centrally planned economy, investment, cycles). 2 vols. Budapest: Közgazdasági és Jogi Könyvkiadó.

_____. 1987. Ciklusok helyett válság? (From cycles to crises?) *Közgazdasági Szemle* 34(12):1409–1434.

BEREND, T. Iván. 1974. *A szocialista gazdaság fejlödése Magyarországon 1945–1968* (Development of the socialist economy in Hungary 1945–1968). Budapest: Kossuth Könyvkiadó and Közgazdasági és Jogi Könyvkiadó.

_____. 1988. A magyar reform sorsfordulója az 1970—es években (The setback of Hungarian economic reform in the 1970s). *Valóság* 31(1):1–26.

BOKOR, János; GADÓ, Ottó; KÜRTHY, Pál; MEITNER, Tamás; SÁROSI, Sándorné; and WILCSEK, Jenö. 1957. Javaslat az ipar gazdasági irányításának új rendszerére (Proposition for a new system of management in the industries). *Közgazdasági Szemle* 4(4):371–392.

BRUS, Wlodzimierz. 1961. *Ogolne prolemy funkcjonowania gospodarki socjalistycznej* (General problems of the functioning of the socialist economy). Warsaw: Panstwowe Wydlawnictvo Naukowe.

CSABA, László. 1988. Mi történt a magyar reformmal? (What has happened to the Hungarian reform?) *Közgazdasági Szemle* 35(9):1041–1058.

CSANÁDINÉ DEMETER, Mária. 1979. A vállalatnagyság, a jövedelmezöség és a preferenciák összefüggése (Some relations of enterprise size profitability and the preferences). *Pénzügyi Szemle* 23(2):105–120.

CSIKÓS-NAGY, Béla. 1966. A magyarországi árvita két szakasza. *Közgazdasági Szemle* 13(4):393–404. Published in English as Two Stages of the Hungarian Debate on Prices. *Acta Oeconomica* 1:3–4 (1966):255–266.

_____. 1969. *Az árreform és tapasztalatai* (The price reform and its concerns). Budapest: Kossuth Könyvkiadó.

_____. 1983. Likviditási gondok és gazdasági konszolidáció. *Gazdaság* 17(2):5–15. Published in English as Liquidity Troubles and Economic Consolation in Hungary. *Acta Oeconomica* 31:1–2 (1983):1–12.

DONÁTH, Ferenc 1977. *Reform és forradalom: A magyar mezögazdaság strukturális átalakulása 1945–1975.* Budapest: Akadémiai Kiadó. Published in English as *Reform and Revolution: Transformation of Hungary's agriculture 1945–1970.* Budapest: Corvina, 1980.

ERLICH, Éva. 1985. The Size Structure of Manufacturing Establishments and Enterprises: An International Comparison. *Journal of Comparative Economics* 9(3):267–295.

ERLICH, Éva, et al. 1982. *Establishment and Enterprise Size in Manufacturing: An East-West International Comparison.* Forschungsberichte 80. Vienna: Wiener Institut für Internationale Wirtschaftsvergleiche.

FALUSNÉ SZIKRA, Katalin. 1987. Kit hogyan érint a személyi jövedelemadó: Egy további aspektus (Who is affected by the personal income tax and how: A futher aspect). *Közgazdasági Szemle* 34(9):1093–1094.

FAZEKAS, Béla. 1967. *Mezögazdaságunk a felszabadulás után* (Hungarian agriculture after the liberation). Budapest: Mezögazdasági Kiadó.

FAZEKAS, Károly, and KÖLLÖ, János. 1985. Munkaeröpiaci kampányok a hetvenes években (Tensions in the labor market and fluctuations in manpower policy in the seventies). *Közgazdasági Szemle* 32(5):545–559.

FRISS, István, ed. 1971. *Reform of the Economic Mechanism in Hungary.* Budapest: Akadémiai Kiadó.

GÁBOR R., István. 1988. Lépéskényszer és kényszerlépések (Jegyzetek két évtized Kormányzati munkaerö—és bérpolitikájáról) (Being forced to take steps and forced steps [Notes on government manpower and wages policy over two decades]). *Közgazdasági Szemle* 35(7–8):803–817.

GÁBOR R., István, and GALASI, Péter. 1981. *A "második" gazdaság* (The "second" economy). Budapest: Közgazdasági és Jogi Könyvkiadó.

GADÓ, Ottó, ed. 1972. *Reform of the Economic Mechanism in Hungary: Development 1968–1971.* Budapest: Akadémiai Kiadó.

GERGELY, István. 1987. Személyi jövedelemadó, de hogyan? *Közgazdasági Szemle* 34(6):711–720. Published in English as Personal Income Tax: Yes, but How? *Acta Oeconomica* 38:3–4 (1987):275–287.

GÖNCZI, Iván. 1983. A mezögazdsági vállalatok mérete és szervezete. *Közgazdasági Szemle* 30(12):1460–1472. Published in English as Division of Labour and Work Organization in the Hungarian Large-Scale Agricultural Production. *Acta Oeconomica* 31 1–2 (1983):71–86.

HOCH, Róbert. 1967. A ráfordításarányos fogyasztói árrendszerről (On the consumer prices, proportional to input). *Közgazdasági Szemle* 14(1):45–62.

_____. 1980. A világpiaci árak és az árcentrum (World market prices and the price center). *Közgazdasági Szemle* 27(10):1153–1158.

JÁNOSSY, Ferenc. 1966. *A gazdasági fejlödés trendvonala és a helyreállítási periódusok.* Budapest: Közgazdasági és Jogi Könyvkiadó. Published in English as *The End of the Economic Miracle.* New York: International Arts and Sciences Press, 1971.

_____. 1969. Gazdaságunk mai ellentmondásainak eredete és felszámolásuk útja (Origin of the present contradictions of the Hungarian economy and the way to eliminate them). *Közgazdasági Szemle* 16(7–8):806–829.

JÁVORKA, Edit. 1973. *Árak és jövedelmek* (Prices and incomes). Budapest: Kossuth Könyvkiadó.

KÁDÁR, Béla. 1987. A magyar gazdaság szerkezeti alkalmazkodása: Középeurópai összehasonlításban (Structural adjustment in the Hungarian economy). *Közgazdasági Szemle* 34(1):1–11.

KÖHEGYI, Kálmán. 1985. Az ipari szövetkezetek összevonásai a hetvenes években (Mergers of industrial cooperatives in the seventies). *Gazdaság* 19(4):115–135.

KOLTAY, Jenö. 1987. Az általános forgalmi adóztatás helye adórendszerünkben és bevezetésének problémái (The general turnover tax and the problems related to its introduction). *Közgazdasági Szemle* 34(7–8):799–808.

KOPÁTSY, Sándor. 1986. Egy reform koncepció világgazdasági háttere (The world market background of a reform conception). *Valóság* 29(12):1–16.

KORNAI, János. 1957. *A gazdasági vezetés túlzott központosítás: Kritikai elemzés könnyüipari tapasztalatok alapján.* Budapest: Közgazdasági és Jogi Könyvkiadó. Published in English as *Overcentralization in Economic Administration: Critical Analysis Based on Experience in Hungarian Light Industry.* London: Oxford University Press, 1959.

_____. 1980. *A hiány.* Budapest: Közgazdasági és Jogi Könyvkiadó. Published in English as *Economics of Shortage.* Vol. A–B. Amsterdam, New York, and Oxford: North-Holland, 1980.

———. 1982. A magyar gazdasági reform jelenlegi helyzetéröl és kilátásairól (Comments on the present state and the prospects of the Hungarian economic reform). *Gazdaság* 16(3):6–35.

———. 1987. A magyar reformfolyamat: Viziók, remények és a valóság: I–II r. *Gazdaság* 21(2):5–46 and 21(3): 5–40. Published in English as The Hungarian Reform Process: Visions, Hopes, and Reality. *Journal of Economic Literature* 24:4(1986):1687–1737.

KOTZ, László. 1983. Szövetkezeti alapítvány—Szövetkezeti társaság (Cooperative society—Cooperative foundation). *Közgazdasági Szemle* 30(1):85–89.

KÖVES, András. 1980. *A világgazdasági nyitás: Kihívás és kényszer* (Opening to world economy: Challenge and necessity). Budapest: Közgazdasági és Jogi Könyvkiadó.

KÖVES, András, and OBLATH, Gábor. 1981. A magyar külkereskedelem a hetvenes évtizedben. *Gazdaság* 15(4):70–89. Published in English as Hungarian Foreign Trade in the 1970s. *Acta Oeconomica* 30:1(1983):89–109.

Külkereskedelmi árstatisztikai adatok 1950–1985 (Statistical data of foreign trade prices 1950–1985). 1986. Budapest: Központi Statisztikai Hivatal.

Kükereskedelmi statisztikai évkönyv (Statistical yearbook of foreign trade). 1974. Budapest: Központi Statiszkai Hivatal.

LAKI, Mihály. 1982. Megszünés és összevonás. *Gazdaság* 16(2):36–52. Published in English as Liquidation and Merger in Hungarian Industry. *Acta Oeconomica* 28:1–2 (1982):87–107.

LAKY, Teréz. 1980. A recentralizálás rejtett mechanizmusai. *Valóság* 23(2):31–41. Published in English as The Hidden Mechanisms of Recentralization. *Acta Oeconomica* 24:1–2 (1980):95–109.

———. 1987. Eloszlott mitoszok—tétova szándékok (Vanished myths—vacillating intentions). *Valóság* 30(7):34–49.

A Magyar Szocialista Munkáspárt határozatai és dokumentumai 1963–1966 (Resolutions and documents of the Hungarian Socialist Worker's Party 1963–1966). 1968. Budapest: Kossuth Könyvkiadó.

MARX, Karl. 1972. Critique of the Gotha Program, by R. C. Tucker. In *The Marx-Engels Reader.* New York: Norton.

NYERS, Rezsö. 1968. *Gazdaságpolitikánk és a gazdasági mechanizmus reformjai* (Economic policy and the reform of the economic mechanism in Hungary). Budapest: Kossuth Könyvkiadó.

———. 1973. *Népgazdaságunk a szocializmus épitésének útján* (Hungarian economy on the road to building socialism). Budapest: Kossuth Könyvkiadó.

———. 1988. Visszapillantás az 1968—as reformra (Retrospect to the Hungarian economic reform of 1968). *Valóság* 31(8):9–25.
An interview by Katalin Ferber and Gábor Rejtö.

NYERS, Rezsö, and TARDOS, Márton. 1981. Vállalatok a gazdasági reform elött és után. *Valóság* 24(3):9–19. Published in English as Enterprises in Hungary Before and After the Economic Reform. In *Public and Private Enterprise in a Mixed Economy,* ed. W. J. Baumol, pp. 161–197. London: Macmillan, 1980.

———. 1984. A gazdasági konszolidáció szükségessége és a fejlödés lehetöségei. *Gazdaság* 18(1):25–43. Published in English as The Necessity for Consolidation of The Economy and the Possibility of Development in Hungary. *Acta Oeconomica* 32:1–2 (1984):1–19.

PÉTER, György. 1954. A gazdaságosság jelentöségéröl és szerepéröl a népgazdaság tervszerü irányításában (The significance and role of efficiency in the management of planned economies). *Közgazdasági Szemle* 1(3):300–324.

———. 1956. *A gazdaságosság és jövedelmezöség jelentösége a tervgazdálkodásban* (The significance of efficiency and profitability in a planned economy). Budapest: Közgazdasági és Jogi Könyvkiadó.

PETÖ, Iván, and SZAKÁCS, Sándor. 1985. *A hazai gazdaság négy évtizedének története: 1945–1985* (History of four decades of the Hungarian economy: 1945–1985). Vol. 1. Budapest: Közgazdasági és Jogi Könyvkiadó.

Plan Econ Report. 1987. 3:14–15 (April 10).

RÁCZ, László. 1980. Az új árrendszer (The new price system). *Közgazdasági Szemle* 27(2):129–141.

RÁNKI, György. 1963. *Magyarország gazdasága az elsö három éves terv idöszakában 1947–1949* (The Hungarian economy in the period of the first three-year plan). Budapest: Közgazdasági és Jogi Könyvkiadó.

RÉVÉSZ, Gábor. 1972. *A vállalati kollektív érdekeltség jövedelemszabályozási és gazdálkodási problémái.* Budapest: Közgazdasági és Jogi Könyvkiadó. A shortened version was published in English as *Enterprise Income Regulation.* Studies no. 10. Budapest, Institute of Economics HAS, 1974.

———. 1985a. Gazdaságunk közvetlenül piaci szektorának kiterjedéséröl és müködéséröl. *Gazdaság* 19(4):90–105. Published in English as On the Expansion and Functioning of the Direct Market Sector of the Hungarian Economy. *Acta Oeconomica* 36:1–2 (1986):105–121.

———. 1985b. The Origins and Development of the Model of Socialist Economy. In *Socialist Economy and Economic Policy: Esays in Honour of F. Levcik,* ed. G. Fink, pp. 21–30. Vienna: Springer-Verlag.

———. 1986a. Bérezés az 1980—as évek Magyarországán (Wage payment in Hungary in the eighties). *Közgazdasági Szemle* 33(7–8):809–824.

———. 1986b. Munkaeröpiac az 1980—as években Magyarországon (The labor market in Hungary in the eighties). *Gazdaság* 20(3):71–85.

———. 1988. A gazdasági reform eltorzulásának folyamata (The process of distortion of economic reform). *Közgazdasági Szemle* 35(6):661–673.

ROTT, Nándor. 1986. Vagyonérdekeltség és pénzügyi mechanizmus (Interest in company assets and the financial mechanism). *Közgazdasági Szemle* 33(9):1099–1108.

SÁRKÖZY, Tamás. 1982. A tulajdonosi szervezet kérdései. *Gazdaság* 16(3):59–87. Published in English as Problems of Social Ownership and of the Proprietory Organization. *Acta Oeconomica* 29:3–4(1982):225–257.

———. 1986. *Egy gazdasági szervezeti reform sodrában* (In the drift of an economic organization's reform). Budapest: Magvetö.

SIK, György. 1966. A tervezés tudományos színvonalának és a gazdaságirányítás reformjának kapcsolata (Relation between the scientifc character of planning and the reform of economic management). *Közgazdasági Szemle* 13(4):405–416.

SIPOS, Aladár, and HALMAI, Péter. 1988. *Válaszúton az agrárpolitika: A mezögazdaság szervezeti rendszere a reformfolyamatban* (Agriculture at a crossroads: The organizational system of agriculture in the reform process). Budapest: Közgazdasági és Jogi Könyvkiadó.

Statistical Yearbook 1987. 1988. Budapest: Hungarian Central Statistical Office.

Statisztikai Évkönyv (Statistical yearbooks). Annual. Budapest: Központi Statisztikai Hivatal.

SZABÓ, Kálmán. 1985. Vagyonérdekeltség és gazdasági mechanizmus (Interest in capital assets and the economic mechanism). *Közgazdasági Szemle* 32(12):1409–1423.

SZABÓ, Kálmán, and MANDEL, Miklós. 1966. Az állóeszközgazdálkodás helye az új mechanizmusban. *Közgazdasági Szemle* 13(5):525–538. Published in English as Management of Fixed Assets in the New Economic Mechanism. *Acta Oeconomica* 1:3–4 (1966):285–298.

SZALAY, Erzsébet. 1982. A reformfolyamat és a nagyvállalatok. *Valóság* 25(5):23–35. Published in English as The New Stage of the Reform Process in Hungary and the Large Enterprises. *Acta Oeconomica* 29:1–2 (1982):25–46.

SZAMUELY, László. 1971. *Az elsö szocialista gazdasági mechanizmusok.* Budapest: Közgazdasági és Jogi Könyvkiadó. Published in English as *First Models of the Socialist Economic Systems.* Budapest: Akadémiai Kiadó, 1974.

SZAMUELY, László, ed. 1986. *A magyar közgazdasági gondolat fejlödése 1954–1978* (Development of Hungarian economic thought 1954–1978). Budapest: Közgazdasági és Jogi Könyvkiadó.

TALLÓS, György. 1968. *A gazdaságirányítási reform a külkereskedelemben* (The reform of management in foreign trade). Budapest: Közgazdasági és Jogi Könyvkiadó.

TARDOS, Márton. 1972. A gazdasági verseny problémái hazánkban (Problems of economic competition in Hungary). *Közgazdasági Szemle* 19(7–8):911–927.

―――. 1985. A szabályozott piac kialakulásának feltételei. *Közgazdasági Szemle* 32(11):1281–1298. Published in English as The Conditions of Developing a Regulated Market. *Acta Oeconomica* 36:1–2 (1986):67–90.

―――. 1987. Vállalati tulajdon, vagyonérdekeltség, tökepiac (Company property, weatlh interestedness, capital market). *Külgazdaság* 31(3):3–11.

―――. 1988a. A gazdasági szervezetek és a tulajdon (Economic organizations and ownership). *Gazdaság* 22(3):7–21.

―――. 1988b. A tulajdon (Ownership-property relations). *Közgazdasági Szemle* 35(12):1405–1422.

TIMÁR, János, ed. 1981. *Munkagazdaságtan* (Economics of labor). Budapest: Közgazdasági és Jogi Könyvkiadó.

TISZAI, István, and MADARSI, Attila. 1968. *A beruházások új rendszere* (The new system for investment). Budapest: Közgazdasági és Jogi Könyvkiadó.

TOLNAI, György. 1968. *A gazdaságirányítási reform a külkereskedelemben* (The reform of the management system in foreign trade). Budapest: Közgazdasági és Jogi Könyvkiadó.

TÓTH A., Ernö. 1982. A mezögazdasági kistermelés árútermelési tendenciái, jövedelme és annak szabályozása (On production in the household plots). *Közgazdasági Szemle* 29(9):1056–1063.

UNGVÁRSZKI, Ágnes. 1986. Gazdaságpolitikai ciklusok Magyarországon: Kézirat (Cycles of economic policy in Hungary). Manuscript. Budapest: Magyar Tudományos Akadémia Közgazdaságtudományi Intézete.

VINCZE, Imre. 1970. Ár—és adórendszerünk továbbfejlesztésének néhány kérdése (Some problems in further developing the Hungarian price and taxation systems). *Közgazdasági Szemle* 17(6):657–674.

WILCSEK, Jenö. 1972. Bérszabályozás és nyereség (Wage regulation and profit). *Közgazdasági Szemle* 19(1):12–22.

Additional Readings

Acta Oeconomica. This English-language journal, published in Hungary, contains many articles on Hungary's economic reform and performance.

ADAM, Jan. 1987. The Hungarian Economic Reform in the 1980s. *Soviet Studies* (October).

_____. 1989. Work Teams: A New Phenomenon in Income Distribution in Hungary. *Comparative Economic Studies* 31:1 (Spring).

ANDREFF, Wladimir. 1988. De Quelques malentendus a propos de la reforme economique en Hongrie. *Cahiers Lillois d'Economie et de Sociologie,* no. 12.

BALASSA, Bela. 1959. *The Hungarian Experience in Economic Planning.* New Haven: Yale University Press.

BAUER, Tamas. 1988a. Economic Reforms Within and Beyond the State Sector in Hungary. *American Economic Review* 78:2 (May).

_____. 1988b. Hungarian Economic Reform in East European Perspective. *Eastern European Politics and Societies* (Fall).

BEREND, T. Ivan and RANKI, Gyorgy. 1982. *The European Periphery and Industrialization, 1790–1914.* Cambridge: Cambridge University Press.

COMISSO, Ellen, and MARER, Paul. 1986. The Economics and Politics of Reform in Hungary. *International Organization* 40:2 (Spring).

Eastern European Economics: A Journal of Translations. Often contains translated articles from the Hungarian literature dealing with reforms. For example, most of the summer 1988 issue is devoted to this topic and includes the reform recommendations of an eminent group of Hungarian economists.

FRIEDLANDER, Michael. 1988. More Austerity and More Reform Announced in Hungary. In Hubert Gabrish, ed., *Economic Reforms in Eastern Europe and the Soviet Union.* Boulder, CO: Westview Press.

GATI, Charles. 1986. *Hungary and the Soviet Bloc.* Durham: Duke University Press.

_____. 1989. Reforming Communist Systems: Lessons from the Hungarian Experience. In William E. Griffith, ed., *Central and Western Europe: The Opening Curtain.* Boulder, CO: Westview Press.

GROTHUSEN, Detlev, ed. 1986. *Hungary: Handbook on South Eastern Europe.* Vol. 5. Göttingen: Vandenhoeck and Ruprecht.

HARE, Paul G. 1988. Industrial Development of Hungary Since World War II. *Eastern European Politics and Societies* 2:1 (Winter).

HEWETT, Ed A., ed. 1983. *Hungary: The Third Wave of Reforms.* Special issue of the *Journal of Comparative Economics* 7:3 (September), containing articles by Bela Balassa, Tamas Bauer, Csaba Csaki, Janos Kornai, Michael Marrese, Rezso Nyers, Marton Tardos, and Laura D'Andrea Tyson.

INOTAI, Andras, ed. 1986. *The Hungarian Enterprise in the Context of Intra-CMEA Relations.* Budapest: Scientific Council for the World Economy.

JANOS, Andrew. 1982. *The Politics of Backwardness in Hungary,* 1825–1945. Princeton: Princeton University Press.

KORNAI, Janos, and RICHET, Xavier, eds. 1986. *La Voie Hongroise: Analyses et Experimentations Economiques.* Paris: Calmann-Levy. A collection of articles on the reform by French and Hungarian economists. English versions can be found in *Acta Oeconomica.*

KOVRIG, Bennett. 1979. *Communism in Hungary: From Kun to Kadar.* Stanford, CA: Hoover Institution Press.

MARER, Paul. 1986a. *East-West Technology Transfer: Study of Hungary 1968–1984.* Paris: OECD. In English and French.

————. 1986b. Economic Reform in Hungary: From Central Planning to Regulated Market. In *East European Economies: Slow Growth in the 1980s.* Vol. 3. Papers submitted to the Joint Economic Committee, U.S. Congress. Washington, DC: Government Printing Office, March 28.

————. 1986c. Hungary's Balance of Payments Crisis and Response, 1978–94. In *East European Economies: Slow Growth in the 1980s.* Vol. 3. Papers submitted to the Joint Economic Committee, U.S. Congress. Washington DC: Government Printing Office, March 28.

————. 1988. Ungarns Aussenhandel, Zahlungsbilanz, und Schuldenentwicklung, 1970–1990. *Europaeische Rundschau* (Summer).

————. 1989a. Hungary's Political and Economic Transformation (1988–89) and Prospects and After Kádár. In *Pressure for Reform in the Eastern European Economies.* Compendium of Studies Submitted to the Joint Economic Committee, U.S. Congress. Washington, DC: Government Printing Office.

————. 1989b. Hungary's Reform and Performance in the Kadar Era, 1956–1988. In *Pressure for Reform in the Eastern European Economies.* Compendium of Studies Submitted to the Joint Economic Committee, U.S. Congress. Washington DC: Government Printing Office.

RUPP, Kalman. 1983. *Entepreneurs in Red.* Albany: State University of New York Press.

SCHOPFLIN, George, et al. 1988. Leadership Change and Crisis in Hungary. *Problems of Communism* (September-October).

SCHWENK, Milicent. 1989. Economic Performance in the 1980s, Prospects for the 1990s. In *Pressure for Reform in the Eastern European Economies.* Compendium of Studies Submitted to the Joint Economic Committee, U.S. Congress. Washington DC: Government Printing Office.

SINOR, Denis, ed. 1977. *Modern Hungary.* Bloomington: Indiana University Press.

VAN NESS, Peter, ed. 1989. *Market Reforms in Socialist Societies: Comparing China and Hungary.* Boulder, CO: Lynne Rienner.

VOLGYES, Ivan. 1984. Kadar's Hungary in the Twilight Era. *Current History* (November).

_____ . 1987. *Politics in Eastern Europe*. Chicago: Dorsey.

VOLGYES, Ivan, and GILBERG, Trond, eds. 1989. *Before the Storm Breaks: The Extent, Limits, and Dangers of Refom in Communist Hungary*. New York: Paragon House.

World Bank. 1984. *Hungary: Economic Developments and Reform*. Washington DC: World Bank.

Index

Unemployment, 134
Union of University Teachers (UUT),
134–135
United States, 85
  Overseas Private Investment
    Corporation (OPIC), 132
UUT. *See* Union of University
  Teachers

Vargha, János, 128
Videoton Electronics Company, 136
Videoton Works Ltd., 136
Vietnam, 27, 37

Wages, 41–42, 44, 46, 75–77, 90–
  92, 97, 143

economic consolidation and, 101–
  102, 104, 106, 107(& table)
liberalization of, 151
profits and, 75–77
See also Income
War communism, 56–57
Wealth distribution, 18–20, 29
Western European Union, 37
Wholesaling, 62
Workforce. *See* Labor
World War II, 22–23, 31

Yalta Conference, xiii, 28
Yugoslavia, 2, 30, 41, 59, 80